WORLD WAR II

1939 – 1945 DAY BY DAY

WWII CHRONICLES

Contents

Every effort has been taken to cross-reference events and key dates for inclusion in this publication, however the author is reliant on source information. Any errors or omissions shall be noted and rectified.

Published by World Publications Group, Inc.
140 Laurel Street
East Bridgewater, MA 02333
www.wrldpub.com

© Instinctive Product Development 2013

Packaged by Instinctive Product Development for World Publications Group, Inc.

Printed in China

ISBN: 978-1-4643-0300-5

Designed by: BrainWave

Creative Director: Kevin Gardner

Written by: Morgan Servin

Images courtesy of Mary Evans Picture Library, PA Photos, and Mirrorpix

www.maryevans.com

Introduction

The 20th century had already witnessed the unbelievable suffering caused by World War I, yet within little more than 20 years another global conflict had arisen from the ashes of the Treaty of Versailles. In reality, the embers were smoldering as far back as September 1931 when Japan invaded Manchuria and they followed this with an attack on China in July 1937.

By this time, Italy had conquered Ethiopia (May 1936 – and would go on to claim Albania as its own in April 1939) and before long Germany had annexed Austria in the Anschluss of March 1938. Adolf Hitler, who had slowly been consolidating his position of power throughout the 1930s, bullied Czechoslovakia into handing over control of its Sudetenland in

■ ABOVE: **The Treaty of Versailles is signed on June 28, 1919.**

October 1938, before invading the country completely the following March so that Czechoslovakia ceased to exist by the time World War II broke out.

Several countries had been agreeing alliances through the latter half of the 1930s, with Germany and Italy announcing the Rome-Berlin Axis in November 1936 while Germany and Japan signed the Anti-Comintern Pact (directed against Communism) later that same month. France and Great Britain agreed in March 1939 to guarantee the safety of Poland but, in reality, these two European giants were out to avoid war at any cost so they failed to take action until it was absolutely imperative.

Hitler's announcement on August 23, 1939, that he had signed a non-aggression treaty with the Soviet Union stunned the world; he was safe in the knowledge that he could invade Poland without any Soviet reprisals. This attack was originally planned to commence on August 26, but Britain announced the agreement of a formal alliance with Poland the previous day. Hitler anxiously delayed the start of the Third Reich campaign… but not for long.

World War II – Day By Day has been divided into the four seasons – Spring (March 21-June 20), Summer (June 21-September 22), Fall (September 23-December 20), and Winter (December 21-March 20) – and takes you on a journey through World War II.

■ **RIGHT:** Adolf Hitler planned to invade Poland in August 1939 but delayed the start of the Third Reich campaign… not for long.

■ **BELOW:** Neville Chamberlain arrives at the Führerhaus, Munich, for the four-power conference with Adolf Hitler, Édouard Daladier, and Benito Mussolini where the representatives of the four powers sought agreement over Czechoslovakia, 1938.

Summer 1939

September

1 The world wakes up to the news that 62 German divisions and 1,300 aircraft had begun the invasion of Poland at 6.00am. The invaders had fabricated news of Polish troops crossing their border to justify their aggression. Germany's two-pronged attack was launched from Prussia in the north and Slovakia in the south – by 8.00pm Poland asked for assistance from Britain and France.

Many European countries – including Estonia, Finland, Latvia, Lithuania, Norway, and Switzerland – declare their intention to remain neutral.

The British government implements Operation Pied Piper, the relocation of an eventual 3.75 million civilians from areas at risk of bombing.

3 With Germany ignoring a British ultimatum to cease all hostilities against Poland by 11.00am, Prime Minister Neville Chamberlain declares war. France, Australia, and New Zealand make the same declaration against Germany.

The SS *Athenia* becomes the first casualty of World War II when the British liner – en route from Glasgow to Montreal – is torpedoed by the German submarine *U-30* and sinks with the loss of more than 100 civilian lives.

4 Royal Air Force (RAF) planes attack German Navy vessels in the Heligoland Bight.

5 The United States announces its neutrality.

■ **ABOVE: The German invasion of Poland using 45 German divisions and an aerial attack. By September 20, only Warsaw held out; final surrender came just days later.**

■ **BELOW: Survivors from the torpedoed liner SS *Athenia* are brought ashore after it was attacked by a German U-boat on the first day that Britain had been at war.**

6 The Polish Army is in retreat, with German forces capturing Kraków.

7 French forces advance into Germany but the Saar Offensive proves to be a token gesture as the operation near Saarbrücken stalls two days later with the troops retreating the following week.

8 German tanks reach the outskirts of Warsaw.

The British government announces its blockade of German shipping and a return to merchant ships being protected in a convoy.

10 Canada declares war on Nazi Germany.

17 The aircraft carrier HMS *Courageous* is the first British warship to be sunk in the conflict after being hit by two torpedoes fired from *U-29* off the coast of Ireland.

The Soviet Union invasion and occupation of eastern Poland begins, leading to Vyacheslav

Molotov (the Soviet Foreign Minister) declaring the end of the Polish government.

The Imperial Japanese Army attacks the Chinese city of Changsha but the operation is doomed to failure when the

National Revolutionary Army cuts off supply routes.

19 Poland suffers a major setback when around 100,000 soldiers surrender to the invading German troops.

■ **BELOW: Polish surrender during World War II. A Polish delegation with President of Warsaw Stefan Starzynski (second from left).**

Fall 1939

■ **ABOVE: The Luftwaffe launched an aerial bombardment on Warsaw in 1939.**

September

25 With Warsaw now isolated, the Luftwaffe launches a massive aerial bombardment against the Polish capital, with an infantry assault taking place the following day.

27 German guns on the Siegfried Line begin firing on French villages behind the Maginot Line (the defensive line constructed by the French between 1930-40).

Members of the Polish government flee to Romania to begin their exile as Warsaw surrenders, resulting in Poland being divided between Germany and the Soviet Union.

While Estonia signs a 10-year Mutual Assistance Pact with the Soviet Union, Soviet troops congregate on the Latvian border.

October

2 US President Franklin D. Roosevelt announces the formation of the Pan-American Security Zone – a region of the Atlantic adjacent to the Americas in which belligerent acts against convoys would not be tolerated – as set out in the Declaration of Panama.

Latvia finds itself under pressure to allow Soviet military bases in their country or face occupation by force.

3 It is the Lithuanians' turn to consider the Soviet Union's "request" for military bases.

Britain moves troops nearer to the Belgian border in anticipation of a German invasion. By October 11, an estimated 158,000 British troops would be in France.

5 Latvia agrees a Mutual Assistance Pact with the Soviet Union; Lithuania follows suit five days later.

The British and French navies form eight groups tasked with hunting down the German cruiser *Admiral Graf Spee* in the South Atlantic.

6 His initial objective achieved with the surrender of the last organized Polish forces, Hitler voices his preference for peace with Britain and France during a speech in the Reichstag (the seat of the German Parliament).

9 Hitler orders his commanders to prepare for the invasion of France, Belgium, Luxembourg, and the Netherlands, while Germany's naval leaders suggest, the following day, the need to also occupy Norway.

10 Chamberlain declines Hitler's offer of peace, with French Prime Minister Édouard Daladier announcing the same verdict two days later.

12 SS-Hauptsturmführer Adolf Eichmann begins his task of deporting Austrian and Czechoslovakian Jews into Poland.

Finland, meanwhile, are the next nation to receive Soviet demands for military footing in their country. The Soviet Union offers to exchange some territories in order to secure added protection for Leningrad.

14 HMS *Royal Oak* (a Revenge-class battle cruiser) is torpedoed by *U-47* and sunk while at anchor at Scapa Flow, Orkney, Scotland. More than two thirds of the 1,234 crew are killed, while morale is hit by the demonstration that vessels are not safe from German

aggression even in home waters.
Stalin again meets Finnish
representatives and advises
them that an "accident" might
occur if the negotiations become
too protracted.

16 Germany launches its first air
attack on Great Britain, targeting
ships in Scotland's Firth of Forth.

19 The first Jewish ghetto is set up at
Lublin as areas of Poland formally
become part of Germany.

20 The "Phoney War" begins. In
preparation for a German invasion,
Britain constructs defensive
fortifications while French
troops prepare for winter in the
tunnels and dormitories of the
Maginot Line. It was something
of an anticlimax though, as
the anticipated onslaught was
months away.

27 Yet another European country,
this time Belgium, declares
its neutrality.

■ **ABOVE: The British
battleship HMS *Royal Oak*
was sunk by German U-boats
at Scapa Flow.**

30 Britain reports on the
concentration camps that Nazi
Germany is building for Jews and
anti-Nazis in Europe.

31 Proposals are put forward by
German Lieutenant-General
Erich von Manstein that Germany
launches its attack on France
through the Ardennes rather than
through Belgium.

November

1 Poland is further divided as parts
of the country are annexed by both
Germany and the Soviet Union.

3 Finland and the Soviet Union
are still deadlocked over
border negotiations, with the
Finns refusing to concede any
territory that might weaken their
defensive capability.

4 The United States signs the
Neutrality Act that allows for
Britain and France to buy arms
but only on a cash basis.

■ **ABOVE: President Franklin D. Roosevelt is shown signing the Neutrality Act in the White House, Washington, on November 4, 1939.**

■ **RIGHT: Officers and men of the Royal Air Force being presented to King George VI during the king's visit to the RAF in France, December 10, 1939.**

5 The Swedish government protests against the enlargement of Germany's minefields, which are now less than three miles off the Swedish coastline.

8 A bomb explodes after Hitler makes a speech in Munich's Bürgerbräukeller. Fortunately, for the German leader, he had already left the beer house; nine people are killed and more than 60 injured in the explosion.

13 The first German bombs are dropped on British soil during attacks on the Shetlands, but the Scottish islands escape damage.
    The Finn and Soviet Union delegations are unable to come to an agreement, leading to the negotiations breaking down.

17 The *Admiral Graf Spee* returns to the Atlantic, having forayed into the Indian Ocean and covered around 30,000 nautical miles.

20 German forces in the form of Luftwaffe aircraft and Kriegsmarine

U-boats start to mine the Thames estuary.

21 Britain (and, a day later, France) announces that exports of German origin or ownership will be seized by naval vessels in response to Germany's violation of international marine law.

24 The city of Nanning in southern China falls to the Japanese.

26 Relationships between Finland and the Soviet Union deteriorate when the Soviets themselves fire shells on the Russian village of Manila and blame it on the Finns.

30 Having broken off diplomatic relations the previous day, the USSR invades Finland. The Winter War has begun…

December

1 The Soviet attack on Finland escalates with the bombing of Helsinki and other towns; President Roosevelt condemns the

invasion. With the resignation of the Finnish government, a new cabinet is formed with Dr. Risto Ryti as Prime Minister.

2 Sweden calls up its reserve forces as Germany launches a press campaign against her with partial mobilization taking place three days later.

5 Soviet troops launch a large-scale attack on the Mannerheim Line, an outdated defensive position on the Finnish-Russian border.

8 The first extensive onslaught in the Battle of Suomussalmi begins with Soviet forces advancing toward their target of Oulu, which would have divided Finland in two and cut off a vital rail link with Sweden.

10 King George VI returns to London

18 German planes defeat their British counterparts in the Battle of Heligoland Bight, the first aerial battle of the conflict to be named. More than half of the 22 Vickers Wellington bombers that took part in the mission to damage as many German vessels as possible are destroyed.

20 Captain Hans Landsdorff, captain of the *Graf Spee*, commits suicide. He had intended to go down with his ship but was persuaded to look after his surrendering crew.

The USS *Tuscaloosa* arrives in New York carrying 577 survivors from the scuttled *Columbus*. The German cruise liner had been in the West Indies when war broke out and was trying to sail home when she was intercepted near the Delaware capes in the mid-Atlantic.

following his tour of the Western Front that included a visit to the Maginot Line.

11 Following an appeal by Finland, the League of Nations urges Russia to cease its hostilities.

12 Soviet forces suffer defeat despite outnumbering the Finns by around 5:1 at the Battle of Tolvajärvi.

13 The Battle of the River Plate takes place off the coast of South America with HMS *Achilles*, *Ajax*, and *Exeter* engaging the *Graf Spee*. The *Exeter* suffers severe damage but the other two vessels chase the German pocket battleship into the port of Montevideo.

14 Russia is expelled from the League of Nations following its continued invasion of Finland.

17 The *Graf Spee* – forced to leave the safety of Montevideo by international law – is scuttled in the River Plate estuary rather than fall into enemy hands.

■ **BELOW: The German battleship *Graf Spee* sinking after it was scuttled in the River Plate estuary rather than fall into enemy hands.**

Winter 1939-40

December

21 Finnish forces drive the Soviets back 20 miles at Kemijärvi, while the Russians again bomb Helsinki.

22 Prime Minister Daladier announces that the Maginot Line has been successfully extended.

26 The first Royal Australian Air Force squadron arrives in England.

27 Finland continues its advance into Russia and reaches Lake Ruua. By this time, it is estimated that the Russians have so far lost 30,000 men during the conflict on the Finnish Front.

　　The first Indian troops arrive in France.

29 While the Finnish government protest to Estonia regarding the presence of Russian destroyers in Tallinn Harbor, it is reported that the Finns have reached Leningrad.

30 The Finns continue to hold the upper hand, destroying a Russian division (15,000 men) near Lake Kianta while capturing vast quantities of men and vehicles.

January

1 A 10,000-strong Japanese force launches a counter-attack against the Chinese in Shanxi Province.

2 Blizzard conditions bring a halt to the Russian attack on the Mannerheim Line.

　　The Germans are feeling the pinch now that the freezing of the River Danube has severely restricted the supply of provisions and products from the Balkans.

3 At the opening of Congress, President Roosevelt warns that American isolation is impossible and that it should be the country's aim to use trade co-operation to promote peace.

6 The Dutch government publicly states its intention to defend its nation against any attack.

7 General Semyon Timoshenko takes command of the Soviet Army forces in Finland.

8 The Battle of Suomussalmi ends

■ **ABOVE:** These rows of jagged rocks, sticking out of the snow, were Finnish tank traps along the Mannerheim Line in Finland, December 27, 1939.

■ **BELOW:** Finnish ski troops bring in Russian prisoners after the Battle of Suomussalmi, where the Finns took a lot of prisoners and equipment, and destroyed many tanks.

in an emphatic Finnish victory. The retreating Russians are forced to abandon much of their heavy equipment.

Food rationing begins in the United Kingdom. Initially this covers basic foodstuffs, such as bacon, butter, and sugar, but this is followed by everyday items like meat, dairy (eggs, cheese, and milk), jam, and biscuits, as well as canned/dried fruit.

9 The British Expeditionary Force (BEF) in France is reinforced by troops from Cyprus.

A costly week for British submarines with HMS *Undine*, *Starfish*, and *Seahorse* being lost in the space of three days.

10 The Mechelen Incident sees a German Messerschmitt Bf 108 make a forced landing in Belgium due to bad weather. Luftwaffe Major Helmuth Reinberger is one of the occupants, and the secret documents he carried with him are of great interest to the Allies as they detail Hitler's plans for a spring offensive on western Europe.

■ ABOVE: Nazi police chief, administrator of concentration camps, and specialist in Nazi terror methods, Reinhard Heydrich – tasked by Hermann Göring with finding a solution to the "Jewish question."

■ BELOW: Hitler speaks in Berlin on January 30, 1940.

The RAF sends out a large number of reconnaissance planes over Austria, Bohemia, and Germany in a massive survey flight while dropping propaganda leaflets on Vienna and Prague.

14 Helsinki is once again the target for Russian bombers who also hit the Swedish island of Kallaxoen.

With a German attack believed to be imminent, troops in Holland and Belgium – as well as those in the BEF – have their leave suspended.

16 Bad weather forces Hitler to postpone his planned invasion of the Western Front until the spring.

18 Russian forces retreat nearly 30 miles toward Märkäjärvi, while the Finns claim to have shot down 11 Russian bombers. The Soviets respond with air raids over Helsinki and Turku over the following days.

21 HMS *Exmouth* (an E-class destroyer) is sunk by *U-22* with the loss of everyone on board

while escorting the merchant ship *Cyprian Prince* north of Scotland.

The stopping of the liner *Asama Maru* by British warships, and the removal of 21 German passengers who were of military age, leads to formal protests from Japan.

24 Hermann Göring tasks Reinhard Heydrich with finding a solution to "the Jewish question."

25 After five days and nights of fighting, Finnish forces are still holding the Russians northeast of Lake Ladoga. Estimates put the Soviet losses at between 13,000 and 15,000.

27 With Hitler concerned that the Allies might use the conflict between Finland and Russia as an excuse to get troops into Norway, plans are quickly drawn up for a German invasion of Scandinavia.

29 Britain repulses German air raids along its eastern coast from Kent to the Shetlands.

30 At a speech in Berlin, Hitler celebrates his seventh anniversary in power with claims that the first part of the war has successfully been completed. British Prime Minister Chamberlain responds the following day with his own speech praising the rising might of Britain.

February

1 With the Finns still battling heroically against their Soviet invaders, it is announced that British and American aircraft have been operating in Finland for two weeks.

5 France claims that 40 of the 55 submarines Germany had been operating in September have now been sunk.

10 In a new trade treaty, the Soviet Union reaches agreement with Germany over the supply of grain and other raw materials.

12 While Russia continues its attack on the Karelian Isthmus, further offensives are launched around Lake Muola, the Vuoksi River, and Taipale.

14 While the British government encourages men to volunteer to fight for Finland, Winston Churchill declares their intention to arm all British ships to prevent German air attacks in the North Sea.

15 The Soviets break through the Mannerheim Line with their capture of Summa.

16 In a violation of Norway's neutrality, the British destroyer HMS *Cossack* enters Jøssingfjord to rescue around 300 British prisoners of war (POWs) from the German transport ship *Altmark*.

17 While the Finns are still retreating from the Mannerheim Line, Erich von Manstein explains his plans for the invasion of France (through the Ardennes forest) to Hitler.

18 The British D-class destroyer HMS *Daring* is torpedoed and sunk by *U-23* while escorting a convoy from Norway.

23 A state of emergency is declared in Turkey after a Russian detachment is alleged to have crossed their border.

26 With Viipuri now in ruins, the Finns evacuate Koivisto and plan another line of defense further west.

28 The first volunteers from Canada arrive in Finland.

29 A warning is issued by the German press department at The Hague to those countries using the controversial British "Navicerts" (Navigational Certificates). These had been used effectively during World War I and were quickly reintroduced to allow neutral ships to proceed with minimal hindrance, but Germany marked these vessels as suspect.

■ **LEFT:** Adolf Hitler receives Erich von Manstein, the commander of the 11th Army, at his headquarters, "Wolfsschanze."

■ **RIGHT:** Sumner Welles, who went for talks to Berlin with proposals for peace.

■ **BELOW:** German bombers attack the British fleet at their base at Scapa Flow, Scotland, and do enormous damage to naval vessels, March 1940.

returned to service before being sunk again in November.

12 Finland finally capitulates, having suffered an estimated 70,000 casualties. A peace treaty is signed, with the Finns having to relinquish large portions of their territory.

14 The evacuation of Finns from now Soviet territories begins with an estimated 470,000 losing their homes.

16 The first British civilian fatality occurs when 14 German aircraft raid the fleet anchorage at Scapa Flow.

18 Hitler and Benito Mussolini meet in a bulletproof train at the Brenner Pass between Austria and Italy to further their Pact of Steel agreement.

20 Édouard Daladier resigns as French Prime Minister amid criticism about the lack of aid offered to Finland.

March

1 US diplomat Sumner Welles arrives in Berlin (during a tour of Europe) to put forward proposals for peace. Hitler, though, fears his intention is to destroy the Rome-Berlin Axis.

3 Soviet forces claim to have captured Viipuri railway station.
    Increased activity is reported over the Western Front, with British fighters shooting down three Luftwaffe aircraft.

5 Finland sends diplomats to Moscow to negotiate a peace treaty with the Soviets.

7 RMS *Queen Elizabeth* arrives in New York having escaped the German bombing of Southampton by means of a secret voyage. The Cunard liner would prove to be a vital war asset, carrying more than 750,000 troops around Asia, Africa, and the North Atlantic.

11 *U-31* is sunk by a Bristol Blenheim bomber in the Jade estuary on Germany's North Sea coast with the loss of all 58 crew. The submarine is later raised and

Spring 1940

March

21 The former French Minister of Justice, Paul Reynaud, takes over as Prime Minister and forms a new cabinet with nine members being an "inner war cabinet."

28 Both Britain and France formally agree that neither will negotiate a separate peace with Germany.

During the last two nights, RAF aircraft have carried out reconnaissance flights over northwest Germany with, for the first time, three New Zealand Squadron planes taking part.

29 The Soviet Prime Minister Vyacheslav Molotov declares Russia's intent to stay neutral throughout the conflict, although rumors persist that the Communists are eyeing up further territorial gains.

30 A modified Lockheed Model 14 Super Electra aircraft is launched by the British Secret Intelligence Service to fly a secret high-altitude reconnaissance mission over Soviet territory. It is a prelude to Operation Pike, a British plan to prevent Germany being supplied from the Russian oil fields.

April

2 The city of Wuyuan is retaken when Chinese Nationalists ambush 3,000 Japanese troops.

3 The Soviet Union begins the massacre of members of the Polish Officer Corps. Over the next few weeks, the Russian Secret Police would summarily execute around 22,000 POWs.

8 British and French warships carry out a dawn raid to lay mines in Norwegian territorial waters to hinder German shipping. Protests from neutral Norway are disregarded…

9 Claiming that they are protecting the neutral status of Denmark and Norway, German forces attack the two Scandinavian countries. Oslo is reported to have capitulated in one day…

10 Denmark surrenders to Germany, while the Royal Navy secure victory against superior German forces in the First Battle of Narvik. The destruction of the German cruiser, *Königsberg*, marks the first time that a large warship is sunk by an aerial assault.

■ ABOVE: Serious, yet determined, are the faces of this crowd in Downing Street as they watch Neville Chamberlain leave London, England, May 9, 1940, for the House of Commons. The following day, Chamberlain resigned as Prime Minister to be succeeded by Winston Churchill. Less than a week later, the Nazis were in control of Holland and in a position to threaten England.

■ OPPOSITE: Paul Reynaud presenting his government to French President Albert Lebrun at the Elysee palace in Paris, March 22, 1940.

The first meeting of the group of scientists – that would later be known as the MAUD (Military Applications of Uranium Detonation) Committee – takes place as Britain investigates the feasibility of an atomic bomb.

12 British troops occupy the Faroe Islands.

13 The Second Battle of Narvik ends with the loss of eight German destroyers.

14 Allied troops are sent to the aid of the Norwegians, landing at Namsos (north of Trondheim), among other places. The battle for Trondheim will continue for about a week.

Codebreakers at Bletchley Park decipher Germany's Enigma Code, providing a vital breakthrough in counter-intelligence.

18 Wary of events in Europe, Switzerland makes plans to counter any surprise attack.

19 The Netherlands places its entire territory on a state of siege.

20 Romania states that any merchant vessel must unload all their weapons and munitions at the mouth of the River Danube.

22 British troops are reported to be fighting alongside Norwegian forces at Lillehammer.

24 Allied forces are forced to withdraw from Steinkjer due to constant Luftwaffe bombing.

27 The construction of the Auschwitz concentration camp in Oswiecim, Poland, is ordered by SS Reichsführer Heinrich Himmler.

29 President Roosevelt sends a communiqué to Benito Mussolini urging him to work for peace.

30 Hitler prepares his military commanders to be ready for his orders to invade western Europe.

In light of Italy's stance, British merchant ships are advised to find alternative routes.

May

1 Under intense German pressure,

Allied forces begin evacuating Norwegian ports.

2 A fleet of British and French ships is en route to Alexandria.

3 The commander of Norwegian forces in Trondheim proposes an armistice as they are running low on ammunition.

7 President Roosevelt instructs the US Navy Pacific Fleet to station itself off the coast of Hawaii in a state of readiness.

10 Neville Chamberlain resigns, with Winston Churchill replacing him as Prime Minister.

German forces invade Belgium, France, Luxembourg, and the Netherlands. British troops land in Iceland in an effort to protect the country from German occupation.

The RAF launches a first bombing raid over Germany with communication centers being the main target.

11 Luxembourg succumbs to German occupation.

Allied troops are sent to the Dutch West Indies to protect oil refineries on the islands of Aruba and Curacao.

12 The British Home Secretary orders all German and Austrian males between the age of 16 and 60 be interned.

While Belgian troops destroy bridges over the Meuse River in a bid to halt the German advance, the Battle of Hannut begins.

The Battle of Sedan begins in northeastern France, which ultimately leads to German forces achieving their goal of reaching the Channel and encircling the Allies.

13 Germany inflicts defeat on the Dutch at the Battle of the

Grebbeberg leading to the collapse of the defensive Grebbe Line.

French and German armored columns battle near St. Trond with an estimated 1,500 to 2,000 tanks involved.

14 The Luftwaffe carpet-bombs Rotterdam with large-scale civilian fatalities (up to 100,000) and an estimated 20,000 buildings destroyed. The Netherlands – with the exception of troops in the island province of Zeeland – orders that fighting should cease.

Almost 50 per cent (45 out of 109) of RAF planes involved in attacking German positions in France are lost.

15 The capitulation of the Netherlands is complete, with surrender to the invading Germans who now occupy Amsterdam and The Hague along with other Dutch cities.

With rising concerns about Japanese activity in the Pacific, Churchill asks Roosevelt to supply materials to continue the war and requests American Navy ships be sent to Singapore.

16 Churchill sees the situation in France firsthand during a visit to Paris and is told that they cannot hold out much longer in the face of German aggression.

17 Brussels falls to the advancing Germans, with Antwerp surrendering the following day.

18 The Battle of Zeeland concludes in defeat for the defending Dutch and French troops.

19 The French city of Amiens is attacked by the Germans, who surround Arras and reach the Channel at Noyelles-sur-Mer.

20 German forces succeed in splitting the Allies in two when they reach the coast near the mouth of the Somme.

21 Germany claims to have taken Abbeville and annihilated the French 9th Army.

24 The decision is made to withdraw British troops from Norway.

25 As Boulogne surrenders, British and French troops retreat to Dunkirk. German troops are ordered to hold back to allow the Luftwaffe to attack the beachhead.

26 Calais surrenders as the Allies launch Operation Dynamo. Nearly 340,000 Belgian, British, and French troops are rescued from certain death or imprisonment over the next few days by a flotilla of Royal Navy and merchant ships aided by hundreds of Royal National Lifeboat Institution lifeboats, pleasure boats, and fishing craft.

28 Belgium surrenders to the Germans.

June

1 The Luftwaffe carries out bombing raids on Lyons, Marseilles, and industrial sites on the Rhone Valley.

2 With German forces on the opposite side of the English Channel, around 50,000 children are evacuated from danger zones in the southeast and east of England.

3 As Operation Dynamo concludes, German planes attack Paris and drop more than 1,000 bombs on the French capital.

4 Prime Minister Churchill delivers

his now famous "We shall fight on the beaches… we shall never surrender" speech in the House of Commons.

5 A new German offensive is launched along the Somme.

7 A single French aircraft inflicts Berlin's first bombing raid of the conflict.

8 The Royal Navy's aircraft carrier HMS *Glorious* and two destroyers (HMS *Acasta* and *Ardent*) are sunk off the coast of Norway with the loss of more than 1,500 lives.

9 The French 10th Army is surrounded after a German Panzer division crosses the Somme.

10 Italy declares war on Britain and France as Norway finally surrenders.

11 The RAF bombs Italian cities including Turin and Genoa. Italy retaliates with air raids on Malta.

14 German forces occupy Paris. By this time, the French government is based in Bordeaux, having left the French capital and decamped to Tours two days before. With the United States having already offered material support to the Allies, France now asks the United States for help.

15 The US Congress ignores pleas from France and Britain to intervene in the war in Europe.

The Soviets issue an ultimatum to Lithuania to surrender with the same "offer" being made to Estonia and Latvia the following day.

16 With the resignation of Reynaud's government, Philippe Pétain takes the French helm.

The first naval conflict in the Mediterranean takes place with the sinking of British submarines HMS *Grampus* and *Orpheus* by the Italian Navy.

17 Luftwaffe bombers attack and sink the HMT *Lancastria*, the former Cunard luxury liner being utilized as a troopship, off the French coast at St. Nazaire. In the worst loss of life in British maritime history, estimates put the number of fatalities at over 4,000.

18 Soviet troops now occupy Estonia, Latvia, and Lithuania.

The RAF withdraws from France as Hitler and Mussolini consider the French request for peace. French General Charles De Gaulle urges his countrymen to continue the fight against Germany.

■ **BELOW: Standing on the banks of the Meuse River, German soldiers watch from a safe distance as the city of Rotterdam bursts into flames, after a German air raid supporting the invasion of Belgium, May 14, 1940.**

Summer 1940

■ **ABOVE: The armistice of Compiègne, June 22, 1940. The French delegation, with General Charles Huntziger, surrender to Germany.**

June

21 The "Battle of the Beams" begins when Churchill tasks British scientist R. V. Jones to find a way of disrupting the Nazis' radio navigation beam by which their bombing raids were guided.

22 An armistice is signed between France and Germany in Compiègne Forest – symbolically chosen by Hitler as the site where Germany surrendered at the end of World War I – which gives the Nazis control of the north and west of the country.

24 France agrees surrender terms with Italy and a formal ceasefire comes into force the following day.

25 Japan moves troops into French Indochina.

26 The Soviet Union issues demands for the territories of Bessarabia and northern Bukovina from Romania. Despite Romanian proposals for negotiations, the Red Army moves in two days later.

28 De Gaulle is recognized by Britain as the leader of the Free French forces.

With the Channel Islands demilitarized by the British government earlier in the month and declared as having no strategic value, Luftwaffe planes bomb Guernsey and Jersey.

Italian and Allied warships engage in the Battle of the Espero Convoy off Crete in which Italy loses the destroyer, *Espero*.

30 The German occupation of the Channel Islands begins.

July

1 The French government moves to Vichy.

2 Hitler's plans for the invasion of Britain (Operation Sea Lion) begin to take shape.

3 In a controversial attack designed to prevent French warships falling into German hands, a British Navy task force bombards the French fleet in French Algeria, sinking or damaging two battleships, four destroyers, and a battle cruiser. All French warships in British harbors are seized.

4 Documents relating to Operation Pike, captured by the Germans during the fall of France, lead to the cancellation of the mission.

5 Romania announces an alliance with Germany and Italy, while Sweden allows the transport of troops and supplies to and from Norway.

Gibraltar suffers its first air raid, at the hands of French naval air squadrons. The Vichy government severs all diplomatic ties with Britain.

President Roosevelt bans the shipment of materials to Japan that could aid their war effort.

6 Aircraft from the RAF and Royal Navy Fleet Air Arm attack Italian warships in Tobruk Harbor, Libya, and the Catonia aerodrome on Sicily.

10 With Hitler determined to eradicate the threat of the RAF, the Battle of Britain begins and the Luftwaffe targets shipping in the English Channel.

12 The Luftwaffe activity intensifies over the British Isles with raids on Wales, Scotland, and Northern Ireland.

13 The Luftwaffe starts laying a series of mines along the coast of Great Britain in an operation that would last almost two months.

The Vichy government strips naturalized Jews of French citizenship.

19 During a speech in the Reichstag, Hitler gives Britain a last chance to agree peace terms. Luftwaffe planes drop pamphlets containing the text over Britain.

21 Following the staging of Soviet-rigged elections the previous week, the Baltic States – Estonia, Latvia, and Lithuania – "join" the USSR.

22 Britain creates the Special Operations Executive (SOE), designed to attack Nazi targets in occupied countries, and rejects Hitler's peace offer.

25 The orders are given for all women and children to be evacuated from Gibraltar.

It is announced that over the last three months, RAF planes have carried out more than 1,000 raids on targets in Germany and German-occupied countries.

■ **ABOVE: General de Gaulle arriving at his London office.**
■ **BELOW: Two RAF Hawker Hurricanes take off from RAF Hawkinge, during the Battle of Britain, 1940.**

26 The United States takes a step nearer mobilization with the activation of the army's General Headquarters to organize and train troops on the mainland.

27 A total of 125,000 men have now volunteered for the Royal Australian Air Force.

29 It is suspected that Germany has been using seaplanes designated with a red cross for surveillance operations.

A large-scale air raid targets the port of Dover, but Luftwaffe losses are high, with 17 of the 80 aircraft brought down in half an hour.

30 Hugh Dalton, Britain's Minister of Economic Warfare, announces the extension of the British blockade to include Europe and North Africa.

Germany closes its border with Switzerland.

August

1 While Hitler names September 15 as the date he intends to launch the invasion of Britain, Molotov reaffirms the Soviet Union's neutrality.

Italy joins the Battle of the Atlantic with the establishment of a submarine base in Bordeaux.

2 The USSR annexes the former Romanian territories of Bessarabia and northern Bukovina. Estonia, Latvia, and Lithuania suffer the same fate over the next two days.

3 The Italian invasion of British Somaliland begins in the East African Campaign. It would prove to be the only Italian victory achieved over the Allies

without German assistance during the conflict.

5 Mussolini and Hitler meet in Rome; the Italian dictator gives assurances about the commencement of an attack on Egypt.

9 With troops needed elsewhere, Britain abandons its positions in Shanghai and north China.

11 It is announced that 4,000 US Army tanks will soon be en route to Britain.

13 "Eagle Day" sees the start of a two-week concentrated Luftwaffe assault on British airfields.

15 The intense fighting over Britain sees the Luftwaffe suffer more

ABOVE: **Mussolini and Hitler meet in 1940.**

than twice the losses of the RAF.

16 The Battle of Britain rages on but the British use the recently evolved Radio Detection and Ranging (radar) technology to great effect, allowing them to react more quickly to German attacks.

17 Frustrated by Britain's dogged defense, Germany establishes an "operational area" around the British Isles and vows to attack any ships that approach.

18 Göring instructs his fighter pilots to give more protection to the bombers, thereby hindering their capabilities. Over the previous 10 days, Luftwaffe losses totaled 332 aircraft while the RAF had lost 175.

19 British troops in British Somaliland are successfully evacuated after Italian forces take the capital, Berbera.

22 Dover and the Kent coastline come under fire from long-range artillery near Calais.
    An announcement is made that Britain will come to the aid of Greece if she is attacked.

24 German bombs hit a church in the Cripplegate area of London, leading to orders from Churchill to bomb Berlin.

26 Berlin is bombed by British planes for the first time, leading to retaliatory strikes against London.

31 The Luftwaffe succeeds in destroying 38 RAF planes and inflicts critical damage on airfields in southern Britain.

September

2 Britain and the United States

complete the "Destroyers for Bases Agreement" that sees Britain gain 50 destroyers in return for the establishment of US air and naval bases in British-held territories.

6 King Carol of Romania abdicates after ceding large parts of Transylvania to Hungary; Fascist General Antonescu goes on to take control of the government.

7 The Blitz begins as the Luftwaffe turns its attention from military to civilian casualties. Around 400 bombers and 600 fighters attack London and other major cities.

9 Italian planes bomb Tel Aviv (in the British Mandate of Palestine) for the first time, with more than 130 civilian fatalities.

The invasion of Egypt is launched by Italy as part of the Western Campaign.

10 The Italian Air Corps – part of the Italian Air Force – is formed to assist Germany in the Battle of Britain.

London suffers another

■ **ABOVE: The Blitz began with attacks on London and other major cities. Here, the ruins of the Guildhall in London are shown.**

■ **BELOW: An Italian column stops at Sollum in Egypt before resuming the voyage to carry troops to the firing line.**

night of heavy bombing, with Buckingham Palace among the casualties.

13 Italian troops advance from Libya into Egypt and claim the port of Sollum.

15 The Luftwaffe launches a concentrated attack on London in an attempt to draw the RAF out to fight. Rather than being annihilated as planned though, the RAF's dogged defense leads to a British victory, with around 80 enemy aircraft destroyed or severely damaged in what has become known as Battle of Britain Day.

16 Peacetime conscription is introduced in the United States for the first time, with the Selective Training and Service Act of 1940.

17 Hitler decides to postpone the invasion of Britain until further notice.

22 Japanese forces occupy Vietnam.

Fall 1940

■ **ABOVE: Soviet Foreign Minister Vyacheslav Molotov (left) is in conversation with Adolf Hitler in Berlin. In the middle is Embassy Counsellor Hilger, and between Hilger and Hitler is General Field Marshal Wilhelm Keitel.**

September

23 A British naval squadron accompanied by Free French forces arrives in French-held Dakar, West Africa, in an attempt to persuade the governor to change allegiance. Shots are exchanged over the course of two days before the expedition is recalled.

25 In response to the events in Dakar, Vichy France again bombs Gibraltar.

US intelligence cracks Japan's diplomatic "Purple" cipher.

27 Germany, Italy, and Japan sign the Tripartite Pact in Berlin, with the promise of mutual aid giving rise to the term Axis powers.

October

3 The Jewish population of Warsaw is forced to move into the ghetto.

4 Hitler and Mussolini again meet at the Brenner Pass to discuss Italy taking a more proactive role in the fight against Britain.

7 German forces occupy Romania on the pretext of protecting the oilfields from British or Soviet aggression.

12 The German invasion of Britain is postponed until spring 1941.
   HMS *Ajax* takes on a flotilla of four Italian destroyers and three torpedo boats in the Mediterranean. Before having to withdraw, following damage to her bridge and radar, the Royal Navy light cruiser sinks two torpedo boats and disables the destroyer *Artigliere*.

13 The bombing of London continues unabated, with over 150 killed, when a bomb shelter is hit. Two days later, more than 60 perish when Balham Underground Station is struck, and by the end of the week more than 1,500 British civilians will have lost their lives in German bombing raids.
   Foreign Minister Molotov goes to Berlin to negotiate the terms that will enable the Soviets to join the Tripartite Pact. It is a futile exercise as Hitler's plans to invade the USSR are already being made.

18 The Japanese bomb bridges on the reopened Burma Road in an attempt to halt China's trade with the West.

The most successful U-boat attacks of the Atlantic campaign take place with the Kriegsmarine using wolf pack tactics to sink 20 of the 35 cargo ships in convoy SC 7 and 12 of the 49 in HX 79 (both bound for Liverpool from Nova Scotia) without loss themselves.

19 Over the next two days, Italian aircraft bomb Bahrain and Cairo.

22 The deportation of Jews from Germany to southern France begins.

23 Hitler meets General Franco but is unable to persuade the Spanish leader to join the Axis.

24 The beginning of organized French collaboration with the Nazis is set in motion as Hitler meets Pétain (head of Vichy France) in Montoire. Seen by many as a traitor, Pétain is tried, convicted, and sentenced to death (although this was commuted to a life sentence) after the liberation of France.

25 RAF planes heavily bomb Berlin and Hamburg despite unfavorable weather.

26 RMS *Empress of Britain* is bombed by a German Focke-Wulf C 200 Condor and fires break out. Two days later, as the liner-turned-troopship is towed to land, she's torpedoed and sunk by *U-32*.

Italy alleges that Greece has attacked Albania.

28 In a move that angers Hitler, Mussolini begins the Italian invasion of Greece.

30 Greece continues to resist the Italian advance, with Patras suffering numerous bombing raids.

President Roosevelt hopes to boost his re-election campaign by promising "not to send our boys to war."

November

1 With Greece and Italy fighting on the doorstep, Turkey declares itself neutral.

3 British troops arrive in Greece (and Crete the following day) to aid the defense against the invading Italians.

5 President Roosevelt wins an unprecedented third term in the White House (this would be followed by a fourth term in 1944) and goes on to state that half of the United States' war output would go to Britain.

7 The Republic of Ireland issues a refusal regarding any hope Britain has of using its ports as naval bases.

8 Greece emerges victorious from the Battle of Elaia-Kalamas, which effectively brings an end to the Italian offensive in Greece. Combined with their failure in the Battle of Pindus, this ultimately leads to the dismissal of the Italian commander in Albania.

9 Former British Prime Minister Neville Chamberlain dies after a brief battle with bowel cancer.

10 British forces begin advancing from Kenya and Sudan to launch an offensive against Italians in Ethiopia.

Free French forces succeed in obtaining the surrender of Libreville, capital of Gabon.

11 Carrier-based aircraft carry out a first successful attack when 20 Swordfish bombers from HMS *Illustrious* destroy or damage half of the Italian fleet at Taranto. The success of the mission – which will be scrutinized by Japanese military theorists in preparation for their attack on Pearl Harbor – secures British supply lines in the Mediterranean.

12 Molotov meets Hitler to discuss the Soviet Union joining the Tripartite Pact. Among the issues the Soviets wish to discuss is Germany's agreement to the liquidation of Finland.

14 Coventry suffers its own Blitz when more than 500 German bombers target the city; around two-thirds of the city's buildings – including the 14th-century Gothic cathedral – are either destroyed or damaged.

Having successfully repelled the Italian invasion, Greek forces now launch their own counter-offensive and evict the Italians from Greek soil as well as capturing Korçë (a strategically important Albanian town) in little over a week.

20 Hungary signs the Tripartite Pact, with Romania and Slovakia soon following suit.

25 A prototype of the De Havilland Mosquito makes its maiden flight. When introduced in 1941, the versatile fighter-bomber was one of the fastest in the world.

29 Germany finalizes its plans for Operation Barbarossa, the invasion of the Soviet Union.

The Luftwaffe targets some of England's major cities, with Liverpool, Southampton, Bristol, and Birmingham being bombed on consecutive nights.

December

1 Allied shipping suffers in the war at sea, with Canadian destroyer HMCS *Saguenay* being torpedoed

TORPEDOES FROM THE AIR: THE TECHNIQUE OF TORP

by the Italian submarine *Argo*, and British ships *Tribesman* and *Palmella* being sunk by the German Navy. Convoy HX 90 comes under attack from several U-boats when the changeover of ocean and coastal escorts is delayed due to bad weather.

4 The F4F-3 Wildcat enters service with the US Navy.

Greek forces capture the Albanian town of Përmet and enter the outskirts of Sarandë.

5 HMS *Carnarvon Castle* is damaged during a vicious exchange with the German merchant cruiser *Thor*. The British ship put into Montevideo for repairs where the crew salvage steel plates from the *Graf Spee*.

The German battleship *Bismarck* sets sail for Hamburg having completed sea trials in the Baltic Sea.

6 Operation Compass is readied by the Western Desert Force. Aimed at halting the Italian advance in Egypt and forcing their retreat into

ICH CAUSED HAVOC TO ITALY'S FLEET AT TARANTO.

Libya, Allied forces comprised British and Indian troops.

7 The Fairey Barracuda makes its maiden flight. The British carrier-based monoplane bomber would replace the aging Fairey biplanes used by the Royal Navy Fleet Air Arm.

8 Hitler decides against attacking Gibraltar after Spain's refusal to enter the war.

9 Allied bombardment of Italian positions in Nibeiwa, Egypt, begins at 05.00. Within four hours, their initial objective is secured.

10 Hitler issues his Führer Directive No. 19 outlining the German occupation of Vichy France.

11 The Italian 64th Infantry Division and 4th Blackshirt Division surrender to advancing Allied forces in Egypt. The Italians continue to suffer, with nearly 40,000 men either lost or captured.

13 As orders are issued for the invasion of Greece, German troops begin taking up positions in preparation of Operation Barbarossa.

14 Long-range bombers target Naples, Italy.

15 Operation Compass succeeds in driving Italian forces out of Egypt.

16 In response to continued German bombing of British cities, the RAF launches its first attack on a populated area when 134 bombers target Mannheim, Germany.

18 The Curtiss SB2C Helldiver bomber makes its maiden flight.

19 As Greek forces advance toward Italian-held Vlorë in Albania, British battleships HMS *Valiant* and HMS *Warspite* provide artillery support.

20 Luftwaffe bombing of Liverpool claims more than 200 lives and continues for several nights.

■ **ABOVE:** Torpedoes from the air: the technique of torpedo-plane attack, which caused havoc to Italy's fleet at Taranto during World War II. (© Illustrated London News Ltd/Mary Evans)

■ **ABOVE:** A prototype of the De Havilland Mosquito, a medium reconnaissance bomber of the British Royal Air Force, made its first maiden flight in 1940; it was a hugely versatile aircraft.

Winter 1940-41

December

22 It is Manchester's turn to face the might of the Luftwaffe, with 270 bombers dropping high explosive and incendiary bombs on the northwestern city. Over the course of two nights, more than 360 civilians are killed with over 1,100 wounded.

24 The US 1st Marine Aircraft Wing is transferred to the United States' west coast.

28 With Greece now holding a quarter of Albania, Italy turns to Germany for military assistance. 40,000 Italian troops under siege in Bardia, Libya, are bombarded by HMS *Terror*.

Two destroyers being built in Southampton are damaged during a German bombing raid.

29 President Roosevelt reiterates his intention to keep the United States neutral but warns the country to prepare for war.

London suffers a torrid night of bombing – nicknamed the second Great Fire of London – with the Luftwaffe raining 30,000 incendiary bombs on the English capital. Numerous historic buildings are damaged but St. Paul's Cathedral is saved from total destruction.

30 RAF bombers are in action over Bardia, Gazala, and Tobruk in Libya, as well as Naples and Palermo in Italy.

31 A total of 567 Allied ships have been sunk during the calendar year with losses totaling around 2.75 million tons.

January

1 Hitler's New Year's Day speech promises victory on the Western Front.

The RAF retaliates against the bombing of London with a sustained raid on Bremen.

2 Greek forces cross the River Bencë in southern Albania, capturing 500 prisoners during a three-mile advance.

3 The Kiel Canal Bridge in Germany takes a direct hit during an RAF bombing raid and collapses on the Finnish cargo ship *Yrsa*.

5 Allied forces succeed in capturing the Libyan town of Bardia from the Italians, taking an estimated 40,000 prisoners in the process.

6 Irish President de Valera protests to Germany over Dublin's three bombing raids in 24 hours by stray Luftwaffe aircraft.

■ **ABOVE: An Australian Gladiator fighter patrol returns to its desert base after a mission over the fighting line near Bardia, Libya, January 5, 1941, which fell to Allied forces.**

8 At a conference in his southern German home, The Berghof, Hitler outlines the Nazis' intentions to support Italy in North Africa and bring down the Soviet Union, but also warns his leaders to prepare for the United States' possible entry into the conflict.

9 Italian forces in Tobruk numbering around 25,000 are now surrounded by Allied troops.

The iconic Avro Lancaster heavy bomber makes its maiden flight. It goes on to become the most successful night bomber of the conflict.

■ **ABOVE:** An Avro Lancaster of 50 Squadron – this aircraft made its debut flight in January 1941.

10 After four days of intense fighting, Greek forces take the Klisura Pass in the mountains of Albania – vitally important as it enables them to link up with troops on the coast – while the Italians retreat toward Berat.

The British aircraft carrier HMS *Illustrious* is severely damaged by Stuka dive bombers, giving the Luftwaffe air superiority over the Mediterranean.

12 Allied troops are organized in preparation for the imminent assault on Tobruk.

16 German aircraft attack Malta's Valletta Harbor in strength as they attempt to finish off HMS *Illustrious*. These raids continue for several days.

The Allies launch their East African counter-offensive, with British troops attacking their Italian counterparts in Ethiopia.

19 British troops put more pressure on the Italians as they attack Eritrea.

22 Australian, British, and Indian troops succeed in capturing the strategically important port of Tobruk.

23 Pioneering aviator Charles Lindbergh recommends to Congress that the US negotiate a neutrality pact with Germany.

24 Allied forces attack Italian Somaliland as the East African counter-offensive continues.

27 Battalions of US Marine Corps are ordered to the Pacific island of Midway, and Pearl Harbor in Hawaii, by Chief of Naval Operations Admiral Stark.

29 Italian forces in the Horn of Africa face being surrounded as the British advance through Eritrea;

■ **ABOVE: Rear Admiral Husband E. Kimmel.**
■ **RIGHT: Soldiers wait on their Panzer III, on the alert for their deployment in the battle of El Agheila, 1941.**

South Africans gain a foothold in Italian Somaliland.

The Soviet-built Tupolev Tu-2 – which would be described as "one of the outstanding combat aircraft of World War II" – carries out its maiden flight.

30 A costly 24 hours ends during which U-boats attacked convoy SC 19 and sank six Allied vessels with a combined tonnage of more than 33,000.

31 The Libyan port of Derna is captured from the Italians. It would prove a brief reprieve, however, with the Germans retaking it on April 6 and holding it for more than 18 months.

The Eritrean city of Agordat is captured by the Indian 4th Division along with around 1,000 Italian troops and more than 40 field guns.

February

1 Admiral Husband E. Kimmel replaces James O. Richardson – who had unsuccessfully argued against the berthing of the US Naval Fleet in Pearl Harbor – as Commander in Chief, Pacific Fleet.

3 The German Army troops in Africa (later the Afrika Korps) are put under the command of General Erwin Rommel – the Desert Fox.

5 Allied forces succeed in blockading the Italian Army in Libya. The ensuing Battle of Beda Fomm results in defeat for Italy and the surrender of around 130,000 troops.

9 With the capture of the Libyan coastal city of El Agheila by Allied troops, Operation Compass comes to a successful conclusion.

10 The German town of Hannover comes under attack from a force of 222 British aircraft.

The first airborne operation by the British military takes place when Operation Colossus is carried out. The objective is for 38 paratroopers of the No. 11 Special Air Service Battalion to destroy the Tragino freshwater aqueduct in southern Italy. They succeed, but the damage is quickly repaired and it is returned to service.

11 The first deployment of German troops arrive in Tripoli, Libya.

12 Seven Allied ships from convoy SLS 64 are sunk northwest of Madeira by the German cruiser *Admiral Hipper*.

14 Yugoslavia comes under pressure to join the Tripartite Pact.

15 South African troops occupy Kismayo in Italian Somaliland.

Britain severs diplomatic relations with Romania.

17 Bulgaria and Turkey issue a joint statement that confirms their non-aggression policy. Turkey – under pressure from Germany – reluctantly agrees not to protest

against Nazi troops moving unhindered through Bulgaria.

18 The United States creates defense zones in the Pacific and Caribbean to monitor foreign shipping and aircraft.

19 Luftwaffe bombers commence a three-day bombardment against Swansea with more than 35,000 bombs being dropped. By the end, most of the Welsh town's center has been flattened.

22 Three Allied cargo ships and two tankers en route to the United States are sunk when German battle cruisers *Scharnhorst* and *Gneisenau* attack an unescorted convoy.

Representatives from Britain and Greece meet in Athens to agree a plan of defence, although there are differences of opinion as to the best strategy.

24 German submarines score further successes with the sinking of seven merchant ships in Allied convoy OB 288.

The first confrontation between British and German troops takes place in North Africa, at El Agheila in Libya.

25 Vital fuel supplies (around 400,000 gallons) are commandeered following the capture of Mogadishu (Italian Somaliland) by the Nigerian Brigade of the British 11th African Division.

27 Thirty Wellington bombers attack Wilhelmshaven Harbor in an attempt to destroy *Tirpitz* – the second Bismarck-class battleship to be constructed for the German Navy – without success. A further attack by Handley Page Hampden bombers the following night also fails in this objective.

28 Hitler authorizes the formation of the Fliegerführer Atlantik, a Luftwaffe naval command that will support U-boats during the Battle of the Atlantic.
Britain and the Free French negotiate the surrender of Italian troops at Kufra, Libya.

March

1 Bulgaria becomes the latest country to sign the Tripartite Pact.

2 German troops move from Romania through Bulgaria on their way to the Greek front.

4 The British government announces the closure of factories not essential to the war effort.
Operation Claymore takes place with a British commando raid on Norway's Lofoten Islands, a crucial production center for fish oil and glycerin. They achieve their objective of destroying the facilities with the added bonus of the capture of a set of rotor wheels for the Enigma cypher machine.

5 British reinforcements arrive in Greece from North Africa, which will allow Rommel to strike back in the Western Desert Campaign following the arrival of German Panzers.

9 The Italians launch a spring offensive in an attempt to defeat the Greek forces in Albania. This last-ditch effort – personally supervised by Mussolini – failed the following week.

10 The Luftwaffe damages numerous Royal Navy vessels during an attack on Portsmouth docks.

11 The Lend-Lease Bill is signed in the United States Senate, under which America begins to supply the Allied countries (with payment being deferred until after the conflict), effectively bringing an end to their neutrality.

12 With tensions rising, 1 million men are called to arms in Yugoslavia as Germany demands their membership of the Axis alliance.

15 An offensive against China's Jiangxi Province is launched by Japanese troops.

16 Allied troops register successes against the Italians in Eritrea and British Somaliland while Hitler predicts that Britain's resistance would succumb by 1942.

18 Canada and the United States agree a joint defense pact.

19 Prince Regent Paul receives an ultimatum from Hitler that Yugoslavia joins the Tripartite Pact or faces invasion.

20 Soviet leader Joseph Stalin is advised by his staff that the USSR is safe from German aggression until after the British are defeated.
Nazi leaders including Heinrich Himmler and Rudolf Hess meet in Berlin to discuss plans for repopulating eastern Europe with Germans.

■ **BELOW:** British troops raid German bases on Norway's Lofoten Islands, March 1941.

31

Spring 1941

March

21 The Libyan oasis village of Jaghbub is captured by Allied forces from the Italian garrison that has been besieged there for 15 weeks.

24 Having returned from a meeting with Hitler in Europe, Rommel launches his first offensive in North Africa. It results in German troops retaking El Agheila and sends the British into retreat… within three weeks they will have reached Egypt.

25 With the Yugoslavian cabinet having resigned four days earlier, Prime Minister Cvetković signs the Tripartite Pact. Two days later, the regime is overthrown in a military coup that unsuccessfully tries to dissolve the agreement.

27 With the changing situation in the Balkans, Hitler postpones Operation Barbarossa and orders plans drawn up for the invasion of Yugoslavia.

   The Battle of Keren ends in an Allied victory as Italian forces flee toward Asmara.

   Arriving in Hawaii disguised as a diplomat, Japanese spy Takeo Yoshikawa is tasked with studying the US fleet in Pearl Harbor.

29 The Battle of Cape Matapan concludes with Allied ships sinking or damaging one Italian battleship, three heavy cruisers, and two destroyers in the eastern Mediterranean.

30 British and US representatives agree a strategy in the event of America being drawn into the war. As part of this agreement, all Danish, German, and Italian ships in US ports are seized.

31 The German 5th Light Division breaks through Allied lines at Marsa Brega, Libya.

April

1 Asmara, the capital of Eritrea, is liberated by the Indian 5th Division, who capture 5,000 Italian soldiers in the process.

   Eight German merchant ships, that happen to be in South American ports, are scuttled by their crew to avoid capture.

2 With German troops succeeding in capturing Agedabia and Zuetania, Rommel presses on with his intention to control the whole of Libya.

   Allied convoy SC 26 suffers heavy losses when it encounters eight U-boats 460 miles off the coast of Iceland.

3 Commander of the Italian Red Sea Flotilla, Admiral Bonetti – who had refused surrender terms the previous day in Massawa, Italian East Africa – sees his fleet decimated by RAF air strikes.

4 Axis troops continue their advance through Libya, capturing Benghazi.

6 Germany invades Greece and Yugoslavia.

   Italian forces in the Ethiopian capital of Addis Ababa capitulate to the Allies.

   Allied forces retreat toward Tobruk to avoid being cut off by the advancing Germans.

8 Admiral Bonetti concedes defeat in Massawa but the damage has already been done, with numerous ships scuttled in the harbor over the previous week to hinder the Allies. It will take more than a year before Massawa will be fully operational again.

   In order to counter any possible invasion by Germany, the United States begins its "occupation" of Greenland; with the approval of the Danish ambassador, air and naval bases are soon established.

   With German troops flooding through Yugoslavia into Greece, Salonika falls to the Nazis.

10 The German battle cruiser *Gneisenau* is badly damaged by

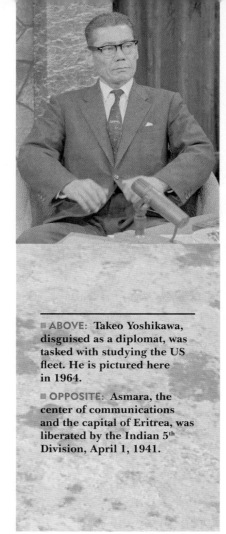

■ **ABOVE: Takeo Yoshikawa, disguised as a diplomat, was tasked with studying the US fleet. He is pictured here in 1964.**

■ **OPPOSITE: Asmara, the center of communications and the capital of Eritrea, was liberated by the Indian 5th Division, April 1, 1941.**

RAF bombers in Brest, France.

The first shots are fired between the United States and Germany when American destroyer USS *Niblack* drops depth charges on a German submarine off the coast of Iceland.

11 Germany's invasion of Yugoslavia is reinforced by Italy and Hungary.

Hitler convinces Mussolini to continue with the war at a meeting in Salzburg, Austria.

12 Belgrade falls to German troops who also record a victory in the Battle of Vevi in Greece.

13 Luftwaffe raids on Malta continue in an effort to secure supply lines across the Mediterranean.

President Roosevelt – concerned by a five-year neutrality agreement between Japan and the Soviet Union – orders the redeployment of naval resources from the Atlantic to the Pacific Ocean.

14 Rommel's Afrika Korps continues its attack on British forces at Tobruk.

16 The Greek Army in Albania is cut off by German forces, leading to the surrender of more than 220,000 soldiers.

Intense Luftwaffe bombing continues over the British Isles, with Belfast, London, and Plymouth suffering devastating raids over the next week.

17 Yugoslavia formally surrenders to the Nazis.

18 Greek Prime Minister Koryzis commits suicide, while the British begin their evacuation from Greece four days later.

22 Protestations are sent to Germany by the Soviet Union regarding border violations that include evidence of Luftwaffe reconnaissance flights over the USSR.

26 Rommel's forces enter Egypt, but his assault on Tobruk will not bring a swift outcome as the siege lasts until November.

27 With German troops now in Athens, Greece surrenders.

■ **BELOW: The German cruiser *Gneisenau* is shown during its test run in the Baltic Sea, 1941.**

■ ABOVE: General Erwin Rommel, 1941.

29 While the last Allied troops surrender in Greece, British troopships are sent to Egypt in response to intelligence reports regarding a German invasion of Crete.

May

1 Liverpool endures the first of seven consecutive nights of Luftwaffe raids that will destroy 70 per cent of the port.

2 The Anglo-Iraqi War begins, with air strikes being launched from RAF Habbaniya, 55 miles (89 km) west of Baghdad.

Plans to relocate huge quantities of food from eastern Europe to feed German civilians and military personnel go ahead despite warnings that millions of eastern Europeans will starve.

5 Emperor Haile Selassie enters Addis Ababa for the first time in five years following his exile after the Italian invasion of Ethiopia.

6 The Luftwaffe agrees to reinforce the Iraqi Air Force, which has largely been destroyed, while ground troops have already begun withdrawing from RAF Habbaniya.

The P-47 Thunderbolt makes its maiden flight. The fighter-bomber proves to be extremely effective in the USAAF's arsenal.

7 RAF Watton welcomes the first B-17 Flying Fortress bombers to Britain.

8 The British seize another Enigma cypher machine and vital codebook during the capture of *U-110*.

9 The Franco-Thai War is officially ended when the two countries sign a peace treaty, bringing an end to the hostilities that broke out the previous October.

10 Rudolf Hess is captured in Scotland. Hitler's deputy had flown to the UK without the Führer's knowledge in the hope of opening peace talks with Britain. Running low on fuel, Hess bailed out of his Messerschmitt Bf 110 and would spend the rest of the conflict as a prisoner of war before being returned to face the Nuremberg Trials.

13 The Soviet Union begins moving troops to its western borders.

14 Manned by American volunteers, RAF No. 121 (Eagle) Squadron is formed.

15 The United States opens the first Civilian Public Service camp for conscientious objectors.

18 Viceroy of Italian East Africa, the Duke of Aosta, agrees surrender terms with Allied forces at Amba Alagi, Abyssinia.

20 German paratroopers invade Crete; within seven days the island is under Nazi occupation.

21 Britain finally sees an end to the Blitz that has plagued the country for more than eight months as Hitler turns his attention to the forthcoming invasion of the Soviet Union. It is not, however, the end of Luftwaffe bombing raids…

22 With the departure of the battleship *Bismarck* and the cruiser *Prinz Eugen* from Grimstadfjord in Norway confirmed by aerial reconnaissance, elements of the British fleet begin to hunt the two German vessels to prevent them breaking out into the Atlantic.

24 British battle cruiser HMS *Hood* and battleship HMS *Prince of Wales* engage the *Bismarck* and *Prinz Eugen* in the Denmark Strait. *Hood* is sunk while the *Prince of Wales* sustains seven direct hits, although the *Bismarck* does not escape damage.

27 Having been crippled during an attack by Fairey Swordfish from HMS *Ark Royal* the previous day, the *Bismarck* is sunk in the North Atlantic by Royal Navy vessels, including HMS *King George V*, HMS *Rodney*, HMS

ABOVE: The people of a be-flagged and decorated Addis Ababa, turned out to watch their Emperor, Haile Selassie, return in triumph to the capital of his liberated country after five years in exile. Mounted on a white horse, the British commander of the Ethiopian troops leads the procession into the capital of Addis Ababa, Ethiopia, 1941.

BELOW: On May 27, 1941, the German battleship *Bismarck* was sunk after a relentless three-day hunt by ships of the Royal Navy. Earlier, the *Bismarck* had managed to sink HMS *Hood*. The *Bismarck* was the pride of Germany's fleet and its loss was a big blow to German morale. Aircraft from the *Ark Royal* slowed the *Bismarck* as the British fleet closed in, finally sinking the great ship some 500 miles west of Land's End. Most of the *Bismarck*'s crew were lost, but these lucky few managed to survive.

Norfolk, and HMS *Dorsetshire*.

31 The short-lived Anglo-Iraqi War is over when the Mayor of Baghdad surrenders to the British.

June

1 More than 750,000 conscripts are called up to the Soviet Army.

5 Japanese air raids target Chongqing in China with bombs dropped on civilians.

6 The defense of Malta continues with the arrival of more British fighter planes.

8 Allied forces, along with Free French troops, invade Syria and Lebanon, currently controlled by Vichy France.

11 Assab in Eritrea is secured by the 15th Punjab Regiment of the Indian 3rd Battalion in a maneuver that secures access to the Red Sea.
　　RAF bombers begin a series of raids on industrial targets in the Ruhr and Rhineland that will continue for 20 nights.

14 RAF daylight fighter sorties begin across northern France.
　　The United States freezes the assets of all German and Italian nationals.

15 The Independent State of Croatia becomes the latest nation to sign the Tripartite Pact.
　　Germany and the Soviet Union begin moving troops into position in preparation for the Nazi invasion.

17 Operation Battleaxe fails to oust German and Italian forces from Cyrenaica, the eastern coastal region of Libya.

Summer 1941

June

22 Operation Barbarossa is launched as Germany invades the Soviet Union with the three main objectives being Moscow, Leningrad, and oil fields in Caucasus. Italy opens hostilities in support of their Axis partner while Romania launches their own attack on southern Russia. The Nazis committed more than 3 million men plus thousands of aircraft, tanks, and artillery to the invasion.

28 Within a week of the German assault on the Soviet Union, Finland joins Hungary, Slovakia, and Italian-occupied Albania in declaring war on the Russians.
    German forces succeed in capturing Minsk and encircle 300,000 Soviet soldiers.

July

1 Operation Arctic Fox begins with German and Finnish troops tasked with capturing the Soviet port of Murmansk. While the Germans accept their failure to achieve this by the end of September, the Finns continue until November.
    Allied forces emerge victorious over the French in the Battle of Palmyra.

3 To prevent the German troops utilizing any materials as they advance through the Soviet Union, Stalin orders a scorched earth policy.

7 American troops replace the British and Canadians stationed in Iceland.

8 Yugoslavia is divided by the Axis countries of Bulgaria, Germany, Hungary, and Italy, although Croatia is allowed to become an independent state.

10 German forces cross the Dnieper River in the Ukraine.

12 Britain signs a mutual defense agreement with the Soviet Union that acknowledges that neither country will seek a separate peace with Germany.
    Vichy France surrenders Syria to the Allies.

15 Werner Mölders becomes the first pilot in the history of aviation to record his 100th "kill." Having overtaken the legendary Red Baron's World War I total of 80 victories, Mölders was seen as too valuable – for Luftwaffe propaganda reasons – to risk any more combat missions, and was appointed Inspector General of Fighters.

Allied forces formally occupy Beirut (French Mandate for Syria and the Lebanon).

16 As German Panzers threaten Moscow, a Soviet counter-attack is already underway near Leningrad.

19 Hitler orders that American shipping is not to be attacked in an effort to keep the US out of the war.

21 Moscow comes under fire from Luftwaffe aircraft.

23 Brest-Litovsk in Byelorussia falls to the Germans.

28 Parts of French Indochina are occupied by Japanese troops.

31 Hitler gives Göring instructions to prepare for the "final solution of the Jewish question."

August

2 Norwegian civilians under German occupation have their radios confiscated.

6 German forces capture Smolensk and 300,000 Soviet prisoners.

US Navy aircraft begin their North Atlantic patrols from their

base in Reykjavik, Iceland.

8 The Soviets lose more soldiers as another 100,000 are taken prisoner in the Uman Pocket, Ukraine.

9 Roosevelt and Churchill meet in Newfoundland to discuss The Atlantic Charter, defining the Allies' goals for the world once the war has finished.

12 The Soviets agree an amnesty for thousands of Polish POWs who form a unit to fight against Germany.

16 German troops capture the Soviet naval base of Nikolaev.

19 Japan stalls as Germany requests they attack the Soviet Union from the east.

21 Hitler orders his commanders to besiege Leningrad rather than capture the city.

25 In order to secure the Abadan oilfields, Britain and the Soviet Union invade pro-German Iran.

27 Comprising Spanish volunteers, the German 250th Infantry Division marches toward Smolensk.

31 The Soviet Navy completes the evacuation of its Baltic Fleet from Tallinn, Estonia.

September

1 The US deploys a fleet of ships – including the battleships USS *Idaho*, USS *Mississippi*, and USS *Missouri* – to patrol the Denmark Strait.

3 The first experimental use of gas chambers at the Auschwitz concentration camp is carried out using Soviet POWs.

4 *U-652* fires upon the American destroyer USS *Greer* in the North Atlantic, increasing tension between the neutral US and Germany.

5 Germany completes the occupation of Estonia.

8 Leningrad is now completely besieged by German and Finnish forces. Apart from a brief respite in January 1943, the siege continues for almost two and a half years.

10 Kiev is the latest Ukrainian city to be surrounded by Axis troops.

11 Roosevelt issues orders for the US Navy to open fire at the first sign of any threat.

12 A renewed offensive is launched against Odessa, Ukraine, by Axis troops.

16 German forces launch an attack on Stalingrad and complete the capture of Kiev (along with 600,000 prisoners) three days later.

18 It is announced by the Soviets that all men aged between 16 and 50 will face conscription.

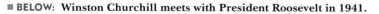

■ **BELOW: Winston Churchill meets with President Roosevelt in 1941.**

Fall 1941

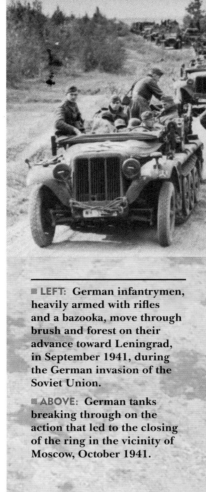

September

25 The assault on Leningrad is halted on orders from Hitler, who instead directs that the city's inhabitants be starved into submission.

26 The Free French government and the Soviet Union agree an alliance.

27 As the weather turns wet on the Eastern Front, German columns have to battle muddy conditions.

29 An estimated 50,000 to 96,000 Ukrainians are executed by Germany's Einsatzgruppen at Babi Yar, near Kiev.

October

2 Operation Typhoon begins as the Germans launch a major offensive on Moscow.

5 Reports filter back to Stalin that German vehicles are within 31 miles (50 km) of Moscow.

7 While Britain puts diplomatic pressure on Finland to stop hostilities against the Soviet Union, Stalin lifts the ban on religion to boost morale.

8 The German advance reaches the Sea of Azov but begins to become bogged down in the treacherous conditions.

10 Over 600,000 Soviet troops are encircled near Vyazma as the Red Army's losses continue to pile up.

15 The German advance on Moscow continues, although the freezing conditions immobilize their motorized vehicles.

17 The United States suffers its first casualties of the conflict when 11 sailors die as the USS *Kearney* is torpedoed by *U-568* near Iceland.

18 As reinforcements arrive in Moscow from Siberia, the inhabitants that have not fled strengthen the city's defenses and await the German onslaught. An official state of siege is announced the following day.

23 German forces thwart the Soviets' attempt to break out of Leningrad.

24 Belgorod in Russia and Kharkov in the Ukraine fall to the Germans.

31 The United States destroyer USS *Reuben James* is torpedoed off the coast of Iceland by *U-552* with the loss of more than 100 lives.

November

4 Kursk (Russia) – prized for its deposits of iron ore – is occupied by the Germans.

5 Japan readies itself for war with the United States if diplomatic relations do not improve by the end of the month.

7 The RAF continues its bombing campaign over Berlin, Cologne, and the Ruhr but suffers heavy losses.

8 At his annual Beer Hall Putsch speech in Munich, Hitler boasts that the war on the Eastern Front is already effectively won.

10 A troop convoy transporting

more than 20,000 soldiers leaves Canada bound for Britain.

12 Both aggressors and defenders have to contend with temperatures of -10°F (12°C) during the Battle of Moscow. By early December, Moscow registers lows of -34°F (-37°C) and some German troops are already showing signs of frostbite.

13 Having accomplished its mission and delivered a squadron of Hurricanes to Malta, British aircraft carrier HMS *Ark Royal* is torpedoed off Gibraltar by *U-81* and sinks the following day.

17 The US ambassador to Japan, Joseph Grew, warns of Japan's impending attack on Pearl Harbor but is ignored.

18 Rommel's forces are pushed back in Operation Crusader, during which the pressure is temporarily relieved on Tobruk.

21 A horse-drawn sleigh returns to Leningrad across the frozen Lake Ladoga with vital supplies of flour, fat, and sugar. Lorries will make further journeys as the siege continues.

26 A Japanese fleet of 33 warships, plus other vessels, leaves the Kuril Islands, heading east into the Pacific.

27 German Panzer divisions arrive on the outskirts of Moscow.
    The last Italian forces in Italian East Africa surrender at Gondar.

December

5 With the Soviet capital just 11 miles (18 km) away, the German assault on Moscow is halted while the Red Army launches a counter-attack.

6 Britain declares war on Finland.

7 Japan launches an unprovoked attack on the unprepared Pearl Harbor. Despite inflicting huge losses on the Americans with the damaging or sinking of all eight battleships plus the destruction of numerous other vessels, the main Japanese objective of crippling the US Pacific Fleet is not achieved. Not unexpectedly, the United States declares war on Japan, with the United Kingdom, Canada, New Zealand, and the Netherlands soon following suit.

8 Japanese forces attack American strategic targets in the Philippines and take the Gilbert Islands.

9 Australia and China become the latest countries to declare war on Japan.

10 HMS *Prince of Wales* and HMS *Repulse* are sunk by Japanese aircraft off Malaya.

11 Germany and Italy declare war against the United States, an action that is immediately reciprocated. Within days, declarations of war are flying all around the world as the conflict truly goes global…
    Japan invades Burma, then Borneo and Hong Kong a few days later.

15 Rommel is pushed back at the Gazala Line by Allied forces and withdraws to El Agheila where he awaits reinforcements.

16 The Soviets take Kalinin in Russia.

17 Allied and Italian naval vessels clash in the inconclusive First Battle of Sirte in the Mediterranean.

19 Japanese forces capture Penang in Malaya.
    RAF Manchester bombers raid Brest, causing enough damage to dock gates that the German battle cruiser *Scharnhorst* is unable to leave the French port for a month.

■ **BELOW: An aerial view of Pearl Harbor (Hawaii), which was attacked by the Japanese on December 7, 1941.**

Winter 1941-42

■ **ABOVE: German and Italian prisoners captured when Bardia, Libya, was surrendered, walk from the waterfront to a POW point.**

December

21 Thailand enters into an alliance with Japan and declares war on the United States and the United Kingdom.

22 With 45,000 Japanese troops approaching, the Philippines capital city of Manila is declared open to reduce civilian casualties. This does not prevent Japanese bombing raids in the forthcoming days.

23 The Battle of Wake Island concludes with the surviving American forces surrendering to Japan.

25 Hong Kong surrenders to the Japanese.

29 Ignoring Hitler's no retreat order, the German 46th Infantry Division withdraws as Soviet reinforcements arrive for the defense of Sevastopol.

30 The SS *Patrick Henry* is launched, the first of more than 2,700 Liberty Ships constructed to aid the Allied supply system.

January

2 Japan captures Manila while Allied troops retreat to Bataan.
Axis troops, numbering around 7,000, surrender to the Allies at Bardia in Libya.

4 The Soviets capture Kaluga, near Moscow.

6 Allied forces continue to press Rommel and advance to El Agheila.

9 Japanese troops encounter little opposition in Borneo and capture Kuala Lumpur, Malaya, two days later.

11 With Japanese troops landing at the Dutch East Indies island of Tarakan, Dutch commanders destroy the 700 oil wells to prevent them from falling into enemy hands.

13 Germany launches a U-boat offensive along the east coast of the United States.

14 Hamburg comes under RAF bombing raid for the first time. The German city will be targeted on numerous occasions with 75 per cent being destroyed.

16 British and Japanese forces clash for the first time in Burma, at Tavoy.

17 South African troops accept the surrender of 5,000 Axis soldiers at the Halfaya Pass in Egypt.

18 Representatives from Germany,

Italy, and Japan meet in Berlin to sign a military agreement.

21 Rommel retaliates at El Agheila and advances north.

22 A mass civilian evacuation begins in Leningrad.

26 The first American troops arrive in Europe.

27 Britain decides to withdraw all troops from Singapore.

29 Rommel arrives at Benghazi, Libya, but the advance is paused as both sides recuperate and await reinforcements.

February

2 Japan invades Singapore with an estimated 25,000 prisoners being taken.

3 The Japanese launch air raids against Java and Papua New Guinea, thereby bringing the conflict closer to Australia.

8 Soviet forces isolate 90,000 German troops near Demyansk who have to rely on air supplies.

9 With the Japanese advancing rapidly, British forces make a last stand in Singapore.

11 Heavy cruiser *Prinz Eugen*, along with battleships *Scharnhorst* and *Gneisenau*, escapes from Brest, evading the marauding Royal Navy. The ships had been subject to Allied air raids so Hitler felt they would be of better service if they returned to Germany.

15 After a fortnight of intense fighting, Singapore surrenders to the Japanese.

16 The Bangka Island Massacre takes place, with Japanese troops killing 21 Australian military nurses.

19 President Roosevelt signs the Executive Order 9066 – also known as the Japanese-American Internment order – which allows the US to declare certain areas as military zones. This order also results in citizens of Japanese descent being placed in internment camps.
  Japanese bombers raid the port of Darwin in Australia, with 16 ships being sunk or damaged.

20 The Japanese advance through Indonesia continues unabated, with troops landing on Bali and Timor.

22 General Douglas MacArthur is authorized by Roosevelt to abandon the Philippines.

23 Japanese submarine *I-17* launches the first attack on the United States mainland when it fires on a Californian oil refinery.

26 *Gneisenau* makes it back to Germany and is safely ensconced in the dry dock in Kiel, but RAF bombers still manage to cause severe damage to the bow section of the battleship during an air raid.

27 Trying to prevent an assault on

Java, the Allies suffer a devastating defeat at the hands of the Japanese Navy in the Battle of the Java Sea.

March

1 The Soviet Union launches an offensive in Crimea.

3 Another Japanese air raid on Australia, the target this time being the harbor and airfield at Broome.

7 The retreating British forces destroy oil installations and military supplies in Burma.

8 The Japanese strengthen their hold on southeast Asia when they occupy Rangoon, and Allied troops on Java surrender the following day.

12 American troops occupy New Caledonia in the South Pacific.

14 Hitler places strategic importance on the targeting of Allied Arctic convoys.

18 Lord Mountbatten is appointed British Chief of Combined Operations.

19 The Soviet winter offensive is halted by logistical and weather problems having pushed the Germans back 100 miles (160 km) from Moscow.

20 Operation Outward commences with the British launching hydrogen-filled balloons toward Germany from Suffolk, England, that were configured to either short out power lines or start fires.

■ **LEFT: A British Lancaster bomber during a night attack on Hamburg. The sky was lit up with search lights and hundreds of tracer bullets.**

Spring 1942

March

24 Admiral Nimitz is appointed Commander in Chief of the US Pacific Theater.

25 More than 250 aircraft from RAF Bomber Command launch a massive raid on industrial sites in Essen, Germany.

28 The destroyer HMS *Campbeltown* (formerly USS *Buchanan* before being transferred to the Royal Navy in 1940), packed with high explosives with a time-delay fuse, rams the dock gates at St. Nazaire… the only dry dock on the Atlantic European coast big enough to accommodate the German battleship *Tirpitz*. Despite heavy losses, the mission is a success and the port does not fully reopen until 1947.

A massive RAF incendiary attack on Lübeck triggers Hitler's retaliatory Baedeker Raids. More than 30 per cent of the city is destroyed, with 80 per cent of the largely wooden-built medieval center being particularly badly hit.

April

3 As around 24,000 Allied troops – comprising American and Filipino forces – struggle with disease and hunger on the Bataan peninsula, they find themselves under attack from the Japanese.

5 British cruisers HMS *Cornwall* and HMS *Dorsetshire* are sunk by aircraft launched from two Japanese carriers off Ceylon (now Sri Lanka).

7 Japanese aircraft bomb an American field hospital in Bataan killing 89 and wounding 101.

9 The Japanese capture Bataan and begin the forcible transfer of POWs to detention camps in what will become known as the Bataan Death March that kills thousands of men.

14 USS *Roper* registers the first American success of the war against a U-boat with the sinking of *U-85* off the North Carolina coast.

16 King George VI honors the resilience of the Maltese people by awarding the island the George Cross.

18 American B-25s launch bombing raids on Nagoya, Tokyo, and Yokohama from the USS *Hornet* 800 miles (1,300 km) off the Japanese coast.

23 The Baedeker Raids begin with the Luftwaffe targeting historic rather than industrial sites. The first bombings hit Bath, Exeter, Norwich, and York.

26 The German city of Rostock suffers a fourth consecutive night of bombing.

29 Mussolini agrees to Hitler's demands for Italy to send more troops to the Eastern Front.

May

1 Japan continues to add more Burmese conquests with the capture of Mandalay and Monywa,

■ **ABOVE: Fleet Admiral Chester Nimitz was appointed Commander in Chief of the US Pacific Theater in 1942.**

while the US decides to evacuate Burma two days later.

4 The Battle of the Coral Sea sees aircraft from Japanese and US carriers score successes against each side, but it was the first time during this conflict that Japanese expansion had been repelled.

5 Operation Ironclad sees British forces invading the Vichy France territory of Madagascar to avert the threat of a Japanese invasion.

6 The last United States troops in the Philippines, at Corregidor, surrender to Japan.

8 German forces capture the Crimean Kerch peninsula from the Soviets.

9 Malta welcomes the delivery of more Spitfires, the effectiveness of which brings an end to Axis daylight bombings. By the end of the month, the number of usable Luftwaffe aircraft in that region will be less than 100.

12 The Second Battle of Kharkov begins as the Soviets launch another offensive. It will prove costly though, with more than 200,000 troops surrendering before the end of the month.

20 Japanese forces now control the whole of Burma.

22 Mexico declares war on the Axis powers.

26 Rommel's forces begin a spring offensive against the Gazala Line in Libya.

30 The RAF sends a first 1,000-bomber raid to Cologne in Operation Millennium.

June

1 Reports reach the Allies that mass murder of Jewish people at Auschwitz has begun.

3 The Battle of Midway – a turning point in the war in the Pacific – commences. Over the course of the next four days, the US fleet sinks four Japanese carriers while losing just one.
   Japan launches air raids against Alaska as the Aleutian Islands Campaign begins. The islands of Attu and Kiska will be occupied until August 1943.

5 British forces suffer during a failed counter-attack on the Afrika Korps at Gazala.

9 The Czechoslovakian village of Lidice is destroyed in retaliation for the assassination of high-ranking Nazi official Reinhard Heydrich.

12 Intense fighting continues at Sevastopol with both Germany and the Soviet Union losing huge numbers of men.

14 With Rommel gaining the upper hand, Allied forces withdraw from the Gazala Line.

16 Allied convoys en route to replenish supplies on Malta come under heavy attack with only two ships making it through intact.

18 The US steps up the race for atomic weapons with the formation of the Manhattan Project.

■ **BELOW: US Navy crewmen are watching as a B-25 Mitchell bomber takes off from the USS *Hornet* for the initial air raid on Japan's capital, Tokyo, April 18, 1942.**

43

Summer 1942

June

21 With the capture of Tobruk and 35,000 prisoners, Rommel – who will ignore orders to halt his advance – goes on to invade Egypt and push the Allies back as far as El Alamein.

23 The RAF is saved the aggravation and risk of carrying out a raid to steal one of the Luftwaffe's new Focke-Wulf 190 fighters when a disoriented pilot mistakes an airfield in Wales for France. The ensuing inspection reveals that it is superior to the Spitfire apart from its turning circle.

27 Allied convoy PQ 17 leaves Iceland en route for the Russian port of Arkhangelsk. Losses are high on the journey with only 11 of the 35 ships reaching their destination.

28 The German forces in the Soviet Union launch their summer offensive with two groups advancing through the Ukraine.

July

1 The First Battle of El Alamein begins with Allied forces defending the Egyptian town against Rommel's attacks. In anticipation of a German victory, British personnel in Cairo start to burn masses of official documents.

4 The inaugural American Air Force missions in Europe are carried out.

9 German forces begin their advance to Stalingrad.

16 More than 13,000 Jews are rounded up in Paris for transportation to Auschwitz.

18 The Luftwaffe Messerschmitt Me 262's jet engines are tested for the first time during a flight.

19 With U-boats becoming less effective against American convoys, German Grand Admiral Dönitz orders their withdrawal.

22 Jews begin to be deported from the Warsaw Ghetto to concentration camps.

27 Allied forces remain resolute and the First Battle of El Alamein ends in a stalemate.

Mass demonstrations are held in London's Trafalgar Square as the public demand military assistance for the USSR.

29 Japanese advances through Papua New Guinea are swift as they reach Kokoda.

■ **ABOVE: An appeal to the Jews destined for deportation to come voluntarily to the gathering places, Warsaw Ghetto, 1942.**

■ **LEFT: A New Zealand machine gun post close to the battlefield at El Alamein, July 1942.**

■ **OPPOSITE: A destroyed Japanese tank during the Japanese push at Milne Bay, New Guinea. Australian soldiers of the 18th Brigade march through the jungle.**

August

1 Chinese leader Chiang Kai-shek agrees to launch an offensive against Burma if guaranteed Allied air support.

5 300,000 Soviet troops are taken prisoner with the German capture of Smolensk.

7 Allied forces begin the Guadalcanal Campaign – the first major offensive of the conflict against Japan – after landing in the Solomon Islands.

8 The Battle of Savo Island sees Japan sink four Allied cruisers in the Pacific.

9 There are riots and civil unrest in India as the Indian Congress Party demands that Britain quits their country.

12 Churchill meets Stalin in Moscow with the unwelcome news that the Allies will not be opening a second front to aid the Soviets.

19 The Allies suffer a setback in Operation Jubilee when most of the troops involved in a raid on Dieppe, France, are either killed or captured.

21 The Japanese attack Henderson Field on Guadalcanal, which received its first American fighter planes the previous day.

22 Brazil declares war on Germany and Italy.

23 The Battle of Stalingrad begins and is one of the most costly encounters in human history with estimated military and civilian casualties totaling around 2 million.

27 Stalingrad is bombed heavily by the Luftwaffe.

30 Luxembourg becomes part of the Third Reich with annexation.

31 Rommel's attempt to outflank Allied positions at El Alamein is thwarted. The Battle of Alam el Halfa is the Afrika Korps' commander's last effort to break through British lines.

September

3 Civilians – men and boys – are conscripted into the Red Army to aid in the defense of Stalingrad.

5 Japanese land forces suffer their first defeat of the conflict when Australia and the United States emerge victorious in the Battle of Milne Bay, Papua New Guinea.

9 Worried about buried bodies decomposing and contaminating the ground water at Auschwitz, the burning of corpses – including the 107,000 already interred – in open pits begins.

The only aerial bombing of continental United States occurs when a Japanese submarine-based seaplane drops two incendiary bombs on Oregon.

12 The RMS *Laconia* is sunk by *U-156* off the coast of West Africa with the loss of more than 1,600 civilians, Allied troops, and Italian POWs. Those that survive face a struggle in shark-infested waters as the U-boat's crew – aided by other U-boats in the area – attempts to rescue them. A US B-24 Liberator came upon the rescue efforts and opened fire, not realizing the U-boats were flying Red Cross flags. Admiral Dönitz would subsequently issue orders banning the rescuing of survivors.

14 Japanese efforts to destroy the United States' Guadalcanal beachhead are defeated in the Battle of Edson's Ridge.

15 With the Japanese 30 miles (51 km) away, US troops arrive in Port Moresby in Papua New Guinea to reinforce the Australians.

22 German forces now hold the majority of the southern half of Stalingrad, having successfully split the Soviet 62nd Army in half.

Fall 1942

September

23 Erwin Rommel leaves North Africa for Germany to spend six weeks recuperating from ailments caused by the hot climate.

Rushed into action months earlier than originally intended, German forces use Tiger I tanks for the first time in engagements near Leningrad, but the new weapon proves mechanically unreliable.

24 In the face of Allied advances along the Kokoda Track on Papua New Guinea, Japanese troops begin to withdraw and establish defensive positions on the coast.

26 Inmates of the Auschwitz and Majdanek concentration camps begin to have their possessions confiscated, with items of value being commandeered by the Schutzstaffel (SS) and the remainder being distributed to troops and German civilian families in need.

30 Eagle Squadron – and its American volunteer pilots – is transferred from the RAF to the USAAF.

October

3 Germany makes a successful first launch of their V-2 rocket at Peenemünde.

7 The Third Battle of the Matanikau on Guadalcanal sees US Marines inflicting heavy losses on Japanese infantry.

11 Four Japanese warships are destroyed or damaged by a US task force in the Battle of Cape Esperance near Guadalcanal.

14 The German offensive in Caucasus, southern Russia, is largely suspended.

16 Luftwaffe air attacks obliterate the Soviet 339th Infantry Regiment at Stalingrad.

17 Daylight raids over Malta are cancelled by the Luftwaffe.

22 The minimum conscription age in the United Kingdom is lowered to 18.

23 The Second Battle of El Alamein sees an Allied offensive opened in Egypt.

The Battle for Henderson Field rages for four days but ends in a decisive US victory that will prove to be the last real Japanese offensive on Guadalcanal.

25 Rommel's recuperation period is cut short as Allied forces advance at El Alamein despite heavy losses.

26 Further naval action in the Pacific sees the Japanese and US both suffer losses in the Battle of Santa Cruz.

31 Allied armored units break through the German defenses at El Alamein.

November

3 The Second Battle of El Alamein ends with the successful Allied breakout (Operation Supercharge), and German forces have no choice but to retreat.

8 Operation Torch is launched, which sees Allied forces invading Morocco and Algeria.

11 Germany completes the occupation of France by taking control of Vichy France following French Admiral Darlan's armistice with Allied forces in North Africa.

12 The Naval Battle of Guadalcanal is fought as US forces successfully set about preventing Japanese reinforcements being deployed on Guadalcanal. Both parties lose several warships over the course of four days of fighting.

13 Tobruk is taken by the British 8th Army, with Derna being recaptured two days later as the Allied advance continues.

14 The Japanese Navy loses two battleships in as many days with the sinking of *Hiei* and *Kirishima*.

19 Operation Uranus is launched in Stalingrad; it is hoped it will give the Soviets the upper hand.

20 The Afrika Korps' retreat continues as the Allies take Benghazi.

27 Rather than join the Allied fleet, the French Navy scuttles ships and submarines at Toulon to prevent their use by Germany.

29 The Allied offensive in Tunisia is halted by German forces in the Battle of Tebourba-Djedeida.

30 The US Navy loses USS *Northampton*, and three other cruisers are damaged, during the Battle of Tassafaronga engagement with the Japanese.

December

2 German forces are pushed back in North Africa with intense fighting in Tunisia.

7 Operation Frankton begins – a commando raid on German ships in Bordeaux. A dozen men in six canoes are charged with attaching limpet mines to enemy vessels in the French port and succeed in damaging six.

8 British and Chinese troops fall back as the Allied invasion of Burma is postponed due to lack of supplies.

12 Rommel's troops retreat to Tripoli and make their final stand at the Mareth Line.

The Germans launch Operation Winter Storm, which aims to break through to the stranded 6th Army in Stalingrad.

The Germans will accept the failure of the mission and the 4th Panzer Army begins to withdraw by Christmas.

17 Large numbers of Axis troops are evacuated from Libya's El Agheila and Marsa Brega regions.

20 The Japanese begin a four-day bombardment of Calcutta, India.

■ **ABOVE: Crusader tanks mounted with 6-pounder guns are chasing the retreating enemy following the Battle at El Alamein in Egypt, November 1942.**

■ **BELOW: Four Japanese transports, hit by both US surface vessels and aircraft, beached and burning at Tassafaronga, about 7.5 miles west of positions on Guadalcanal, November 1942.**

Winter 1942-43

48

December

22 German forces begin retreating from the Caucasus.

26 After two weeks of fighting in the Tunisian Campaign, Allied forces – having stalled at Longstop Hill outside Tunis four days earlier and being forced to withdraw – find themselves back where they started, having lost almost 21,000 men.

31 The Allies emerge victorious in the Battle of the Barents Sea off Norway, which results in Hitler becoming convinced that U-boats are a more effective weapon and ordering that the surface fleet be scrapped.

January

2 Australian and US forces recapture Buna, Papua New Guinea.

8 Axis convoys between Italy and Tripoli, Libya, suffer catastrophic losses at the hands of British warships leading to the supply route being suspended.

10 Soviet troops begin an offensive against the Germans in Stalingrad as well as in Leningrad and the Caucasus.

14 Roosevelt and Churchill meet with French representatives in Casablanca where they discuss plans for the invasion of Europe and call for the unconditional surrender of the Axis powers.

16 Iraq declares war on the Axis countries.

21 Soviets capture the last German-held airfield in Stalingrad, thereby ensuring that no further supplies can be flown in.

23 Allied forces capture the Libyan capital of Tripoli.

28 In a possible indication that Germany has spread its resources too wide, a new conscription law is introduced that means men between the ages of 16 and 65 and women 17-50 can expect to be called up.

29 The US Navy is unable to prevent Japan from evacuating troops from Guadalcanal during the Battle of Rennell Island, in which the cruiser USS *Chicago* is sunk.

February

2 The commander of the last German forces in Stalingrad surrenders to the Soviets.

6 Brazil adds Japan to the list of countries it has declared war on.

9 American forces clear all Japanese troops from Guadalcanal Island – their first major achievement in the war in the Pacific.

10 Soviet troops begin their advance through Stalingrad to mop up pockets of German soldiers still fighting.

13 As they start an offensive to the west, the Red Army crosses the River Don, southeast of Moscow, en route to liberating Kharkov, Krasnograd, Kursk, Pavlograd, and Rostov. The Germans, however, are not completely defeated and launch a series of counter-attacks over the next few weeks.

15 US B-17 bombers launch attacks on Japanese forces in Australian New Guinea.

19 The Battle of Kasserine Pass takes place in Tunisia. Inexperienced US troops suffer heavy losses against Rommel's battle-hardened soldiers during the weeklong engagement.

22 The new man at the helm of RAF Bomber Command – Air Marshal Sir Arthur Harris – is charged with targeting densely populated areas of German cities rather than industrial zones in an effort to destroy morale.

28 The Norsk Hydro heavy water production plant at Telemark, Norway, is sabotaged by Norwegian paratroopers in an effort to hamper the German war machine.

March

2 Rommel is forced to retreat after the Battle of Medenine – it will prove to be his last battle in Africa.

4 The Allies rout their Japanese counterparts in the Battle of the Bismarck Sea. Intelligence reports had warned them of a convoy carrying troops to reinforce Papua New Guinea, so the US and Australian contingents were perfectly prepared. All eight Japanese troop transports are destroyed, along with a large proportion of the escorting destroyers.

5 The Gloster Meteor – which would be the only jet-powered aircraft used by the Allies during the conflict – makes its maiden flight.

13 A plot to assassinate Hitler by smuggling an explosive device onto his plane during a flight from Russia to Germany fails when the bomb malfunctions.

16 The Battle of the Atlantic sees 27 Allied ships destroyed within 24 hours, with eight of the casualties coming from convoy HX 229.

20 Members of the Japanese Navy are instructed that any Allied personnel captured at sea are to be executed.

■ **BELOW: Allied forces operating an anti-aircraft battery in the final drive on Tripoli, during combat on the North Africa front, 1943.**

Spring 1943

March

22 The British secretly listen in to the conversation of two captured German generals who discuss plans for long-range missiles.

23 Dortmund is the victim of the RAF's heaviest bombing raid of the conflict so far when 2,000 tons of explosives are dropped on the German city.

26 Hitler informs Mussolini that Stalingrad is so weakened that it is only a matter of time before the city falls.

27 Allied forces break through the Mareth Line in Tunisia.

29 Hitler instructs missile launch sites to be constructed along the French coast.

■ **ABOVE:** General Montgomery, commander of the 8th Army, congratulating New Zealand and English armored troops who took part in the great outflanking movement which forced the Afrika Korps to abandon the Mareth Line positions. This movement has now become known as "Monty's left hook," 1943.

April

5 Operation Flax – designed to prevent Axis air supplies to Tunisia – is launched by the Allies.

7 British (heading west) and US forces (heading east) link up near Gafsa, Tunisia.
   Bolivia declares war on Germany, Italy, and Japan.

8 The Soviet advance through the Crimea continues through Kerch; the Germans retreat toward Sevastopol.

13 Reports reach the West via a Radio Berlin broadcast of the massacre of more than 22,000 Polish POWs at Katyn in Poland by the Soviet secret police in April and May 1940.

18 US P38s shoot down a Mitsubishi G4M plane over Bougainville in the Solomon Islands that was taking Admiral Yamamoto on an inspection tour. The main architect of Japan's naval strategy is killed instantly.
   Large numbers of German planes are destroyed en route to evacuating troops from Tunisia in what became known as the Palm Sunday Massacre.

26 British forces in Tunisia eventually take Longstop Hill from the Germans en route to Tunis.

squadron breaches vital Ruhr dams

Thousands of gallons of water pour through the huge hole blasted in the Mohne dam by the RAF's new "bouncing bombs".

One of the new bombs is dropped by a low-flying Lancaster over the Ruhr.

The leader of the raid: Guy Gibson.

■ LEFT: The Dambusters raid breached two dams in the Ruhr Valley with bouncing bombs, 1943.

■ BELOW: Rear Admiral Karl Dönitz, commander of the German U-boat forces, is pictured in 1943.

27 The British begin using devices to jam enemy radar signals over eastern England.

29 A busy day for Allied convoy ONS 5 en route from Liverpool to Halifax as five U-boats attack. More British destroyers are sent to the North Atlantic to increase the number of escort ships.

May

7 While the British 1st Army takes Tunis, their US colleagues capture Bizerte, the northern most city in Africa.

9 The Changjiao Massacre is the latest in the line of atrocities carried out in the name of war; the Japanese kill around 30,000 Chinese civilians over a three-day period.

11 US forces land on Attu Island to begin their campaign to rid the Aleutian Islands of Japanese troops.

13 The long North Africa campaign ends as the remaining German

and Italian troops surrender with more than 250,000 taken prisoner. The Allied victory in North Africa enables the invasion of Italy to be launched.

16 The Möhne and Edersee dams in the Ruhr Valley are breached by bouncing bombs developed my Barnes Wallis during the RAF's Operation Chastise, more popularly known as the Dambusters Raid.

German forces occupying Poland end the Warsaw Ghetto Uprising. Estimates put the number of Jews dead at 14,000, while 40,000 are deported to the Treblinka death camp.

24 With 41 German U-boats sunk in three weeks, Admiral Dönitz orders the withdrawal of U-boats from the North Atlantic.

26 Allied convoy SC 130 reaches Liverpool safely without the loss of a single ship. It is seen as a turning point in the Battle for the Atlantic.

30 The Battle of Attu concludes in bloody fashion when US troops kill the remaining Japanese after more than two weeks of fighting.

June

5 The first B-29 bombing sortie is carried out when the 77 USAAF aircraft attack Thailand's capital Bangkok.

8 The Aleutian Island of Kiska is relinquished by the Japanese, thereby ending their foray into the western hemisphere.

10 RAF and USAAF aircraft begin a coordinated offensive on German targets.

11 The Japanese lose all territorial gains acquired since their May 5 offensive into China's Hubei and Hunan provinces.

15 The test flight of the Arado Ar 234 – the world's first operational jet bomber – takes place at Rheine Airfield in Germany.

17 The Allies begin bombing the Italian mainland and the island of Sicily as preparations grow for a full-scale invasion.

20 Shuttle bombing is introduced by the RAF, where aircraft depart from British airfields to bomb targets in Germany before reloading and refueling in Africa to raid Italy on the way back.

Summer 1943

■ **ABOVE:** On July 12, 1943, the two biggest armored combat units to be seen in the history of the war rolled onto the curved frontline of Kursk. Because the Soviet leadership was informed about the time and battle strategy of the German attack, it was well prepared. There was a German order, by which the tank commanders were forbidden to protect fallen tanks and to save the occupants, so that no time would be lost. Despite this, they failed in their objective.

June

27 Repairs are completed on the Ruhr dams damaged the previous month.

30 US forces begin the invasion of New Georgia in the Solomon Islands as part of Operation Cartwheel.

July

5 The Battle of Kursk begins, pitting 912,000 German troops against more than 2.5 million Soviets in the largest series of armored clashes in history. The Soviets had had plenty of time to prepare for the Nazi onslaught and the German war machine exhausted itself trying to break down the defenses.

10 The Allies launch Operation Husky, the invasion of Sicily that is the first step in the Italian Campaign.

12 The Battle of Prokhorovka, the largest tank battle in history, sees Soviet and German armored units engaging during the contest for Kursk. While neither side claim a decisive victory, the Germans fail in their objective of surrounding the Soviets.

17 The US 7th Army captures the Sicilian ports of Agrigento and Porto Empedocle.

19 More than 250 B-17 and B-24 aircraft of the USAAF bomb the Italian capital of Rome, causing more than 1,500 civilian fatalities.

24 A concerted series of bombing raids is launched on Hamburg by the RAF and USAAF. By the end of the week, more than 250,000 of the German city's houses have been destroyed and over 42,000 people killed.

25 Facing revolt from members of the Italian government, Mussolini is overthrown, replaced by Marshal Pietro Badoglio, and arrested.

August

5 German forces begin the evacuation of Belgorod as Soviet troops close in on the Russian city.

7 The United States Navy defeats its Japanese counterpart in the Battle of Vella Gulf in the Southwest Pacific. Three of Japan's four destroyers are sunk, with the loss of more than 1,200 lives, as destroyers are freed of the need to accompany cruisers.

10 The Germans realize that their Enigma cypher has been decoded, but believe the new types and procedures are safe again.

15 With massive naval and air support, 35,000 US and Canadian troops land on Kiska Island only to find it deserted, with the Japanese having abandoned it three weeks earlier.

17 The Allies complete their occupation of the Island of Sicily after 39 days of fighting that paves the way to invade the Italian mainland.
Operation Crossbow – the Allied targeting of Germany's long-range missile program – is launched, with raids against the V-2 rocket facility at Peenemünde.

23 Soviet troops succeed in liberating Kharkov (the country's third largest city) from the occupying Germans who had held it almost continuously since October 1941.

29 Martial law is declared in German-occupied Denmark, while the Royal Family is "isolated for their own protection."

31 Limited withdrawal of German troops from the Ukraine is authorized by Hitler.

■ **ABOVE: Benito Mussolini was overthrown in July 1943.**

■ **BELOW: British soldiers greeted by local villagers during the Allied invasion and liberation of Italy, 1943.**

September

3 Allied forces comprising British, Canadian, and American troops carry out the invasion of mainland Italy. They encounter little opposition and an armistice is quickly negotiated that sees Italy leave the Axis alliance and drop out of the war.

4 Australian and US troops land on Papua New Guinea, with Lae and Salamau being captured.

8 As news of Italy's surrender is made public, German forces begin to occupy the country, with troops arriving in Rome two days later.

9 Allied forces land at Salerno and Taranto with the aim of advancing up through Italy.

12 A German paratrooper operation releases Mussolini from imprisonment to be installed by Hitler as the head of "the Italian Social Republic."

14 The Allies make huge gains in Italy, with Bari and Sardinia soon within their grasp.

16 Following the successes enjoyed in Italy, Allied troops land on Italian-held Greek islands. Unfortunately, they are ousted by invading German forces who would control the Dodecanese Islands by the end of November.

21 German battleship *Tirpitz* is put out of action for six months during an attack by British midget submarines in Norway's Alta Fjord.

Fall 1943

September

25 The Soviets liberate Smolensk from German control as they advance on a 400-mile front.

27 The last German-held port on the Black Sea, Temryuk, is captured by Soviet forces.

29 While the Allies continue to make gains in Italy and take Pompeii, resistance fighters and residents of Naples begin an attempt to overthrow the Germans.

October

1 As the Allies enter Naples, the city's residents complete their uprising against the occupying Germans.

6 The Japanese complete their evacuation of the Solomon Islands and sink or damage three US destroyers during the Naval Battle of Vella Lavella.

8 Allied engineers begin the construction of anti-submarine bases in the Azores in the middle of the Atlantic Ocean. Once these become operational, losses in the Battle of the Atlantic drop dramatically.

13 Italy declares war on Germany.

14 Allied long-range daylight bombing raids are suspended after heavy losses are incurred during an attack on Schweinfurt. They will only be reinstated once P-51 fighters are available to fly escort to the bombers.

20 The United Nations Commission for the Investigation of War Crimes is established.

22 Allied bombing raids on Kassel are so severe that the German town burns for a week afterward.

31 US forces resume their offensive against German defensive positions on the Volturno Line in Italy.

November

1 The Solomon Islands are again at the forefront of the action, with US Marines landing on Bougainville.

3 Franco orders all Spanish volunteers from the disbanded German 250th Infantry Division to return to Spain.

6 Soviet forces recapture Kiev on the 26th anniversary of the Russian Revolution.

15 More than four years after the start of the conflict, many can see light at the end of the tunnel, with the formation of the Allied Expeditionary Force in anticipation of the invasion of Europe.

16 British and Italian troops surrender to the Germans at the end of the Battle of Leros in the Aegean Sea.

18 RAF Bomber Command launches the Battle of Berlin, with a series of raids on the German capital.

20 US Marines land in the Gilbert Islands but come under intense Japanese fire. Around 3,500 casualties are suffered during the taking of Tarawa Atoll.

22 Roosevelt, Churchill, and Chiang Kai-shek meet in Cairo to discuss ways of defeating Japan.

25 The last action between surface vessels in the Solomon Islands Campaign sees a US victory in the Battle of Cape St. George as three Japanese destroyers are sunk.

December

2 Hitler extends conscription to the youth of Germany.
   A Luftwaffe raid on the Italian port of Bari hits an Allied cargo ship carrying a consignment of mustard gas.

8 Royal Canadian Engineers build a bridge over the Moro River in Italy to enable tanks to reinforce the recently gained bridgehead.

12 Czechoslovakia and the Soviet Union sign a treaty of friendship in Moscow.

18 US General Joseph Stilwell is given command of Chinese troops.

19 Lord Mountbatten orders the merging of RAF and USAAF units in southeast Asia into one combined force.

■ **ABOVE: During a RAF raid on Kassel, the pilot of one of the Stirling bombers was wounded and had to make an emergency landing on the return journey at a US aerodrome. His plane was later collected by a relief pilot, 1943.**

Winter 1943-44

December

22 Josip Broz Tito is installed as the Allied commander in Yugoslavia.

26 The German battle cruiser *Scharnhorst* is sunk by British warships off the North Cape of Norway.

27 The Allied advance through Italy reaches the Gustav Line of German defenses.

28 Three German destroyers are sunk by British cruisers HMS *Enterprise* and HMS *Glasgow* off the coast of France.

January

4 The Allies begin to airdrop supplies to resistance fighters in occupied Europe.

6 Having advanced around 200 miles (320 km) in just two weeks, Soviet troops cross the border into Poland.

9 The Burmese port of Maungdaw is captured by soldiers of the Indian 5th Division.

12 Despite severe weather hampering the operation, the US 5th Army captures Cervaro during its offensive in the Gustav Line.

16 General Eisenhower takes up his role as Supreme Commander of the Allied forces in Europe.

22 The Allies land in Italy at Anzio, launching Operation Shingle. The fighting is intense over the next four months but the objective of establishing a beachhead is eventually achieved.

24 Orders issued by Hitler state that the Gustav Line in Italy is to be held whatever the cost.

27 After almost two years and five months, the Siege of Leningrad is over.

February

5 German commanders finally shelve Operation Sea Lion, the planned invasion of Britain.

7 US forces capture two atolls in the Marshall Islands. Further gains would be made over the coming weeks.

10 Control of southern Italy is handed over to the Italian Royal government by the Allies.

15 Fearing that German forces were using the ancient Benedictine monastery at Monte Cassino as part of their defensive line, the Allies destroy the building during bombing raids.

19 The Luftwaffe begins a week of heavy bombing over London while the Allies target German industrial cities.

22 Stalin announces that German troops have been evicted from 75 per cent of the Soviet territory it had invaded.

26 Japan calls off the Battle of the Admin Box, an operation that was based on a counter-attack against Allied forces in Burma, after more than two weeks of fighting.

Commander of the 112th Infantry Regiment, Colonel Tanahashi, had retreated two days earlier without waiting for authorization.

March

2 Egon Mayer, the first Luftwaffe ace to claim 100 victories on the Western Front, is shot down and killed over Montmédy, France.

6 An intense bombardment of France begins in preparation for the invasion of Normandy.

8 Japan launches an invasion of India. The Imperial forces would get as far as Kohima and Imphal before being repulsed by early July.

10 The Soviet offensive in the Ukraine advances toward the Dniester and Bug rivers. The latter was the point at which the German invasion of the USSR had begun.

17 USAAF aircraft launch a first bombing raid on Vienna, Austria, from Italy.

19 With Hungary discussing an armistice with the Allies, Germany invades and occupies its former ally.

■ **BELOW: General Eisenhower became Supreme Commander of the Allied forces in Europe.**

Spring 1944

■ **ABOVE:** Pilots of the American 8ᵗʰ Air Force being debriefed by an Intelligence Officer following a daylight raid on occupied France in preparation for D-Day.

■ **OPPOSITE:** Off the British coast, this huge fleet of warships, transports, and landing craft awaits the signal to get underway for the Allied invasion of Northern France, June 6, 1944.

March

22 Canada and China sign a mutual aid pact.

24 A total of 76 Allied POWs escape from the Stalag Luft III camp in a scheme that was later popularized in the 1963 movie *The Great Escape*. Of the escapees, 73 were caught and 50 of those were executed on the orders of Hitler as a deterrent.

30 RAF Bomber Command losses during a raid on Nuremberg prove to be the costliest of the war with 96 out of the 795 aircraft failing to return.

April

3 In order to aid the Soviet advance through eastern Europe, Allied bombers raid the capital cities of Hungary and Romania.

6 With the war in parts of Europe starting to show signs of an end, the first evacuees return to Gibraltar.

12 The evacuation begins of more than 61,000 German troops in the Crimea.

15 Cracks begin to appear in the German defensive Gustav Line in Italy as the Allies keep pressing.

19 A Japanese offensive is launched in China with the objective being Guilin and Liuzhou in the southeast of the country from where American bombers are due to launch raids against Japan.

22 Japanese forces in New Guinea are now isolated as Americans land at Hollandia and Aitape.

25 The funeral of German General Hans-Valentin Hube also marks one of Hitler's last public appearances.

28 Around 750 Allied lives are lost when US landing ships on exercise off the coast of Devon, England, are torpedoed by German E-boats.

30 Despite the secrecy, extensive maneuvers around southern England give a hint that a major operation (the D-Day landings) is being prepared for.

May

8 With the date for Operation Overlord (the Battle of Normandy) set for June 4, Allied aircraft carry out extensive bombing raids of continental Europe.

9 The Soviets liberate Sevastopol as the German Army retreats from the Crimean peninsula.

15 A German directive comes into force, stipulating that 3,000 Hungarian Jews are to be sent to the Auschwitz concentration camp each day as the extermination process is accelerated.

18 The Allies win the Battle of Monte Cassino after five months of fighting.

20 Polish resistance fighters capture an intact V-2 rocket during testing and later manage to smuggle critical parts to England for analysis.

25 With the Germans now in retreat from Anzio, the Allies can begin the final offensive on Rome.

27 As disillusionment with both Hitler and the war grows, several high-ranking Germans meet to discuss overthrowing the Führer and replacing him with Erwin Rommel. They believe that the

Allies might be more likely to negotiate peace terms with the Desert Fox.

June

2 Bulgaria asks for surrender terms from the Western Allies.

4 Bad weather enforces the postponement of Operation Overlord.

5 Although Italy had surrendered in September, it took another eight months before the Allies were able to liberate Rome from the Germans.

6 The Allies launch D-Day with 4,000 ships landing troops on the Normandy beaches in France as the invasion of German-occupied western Europe begins.

12 Japanese positions in the Mariana Islands are attacked by aircraft from US carriers.

13 Germany launches the first of many V-1 flying bombs at London. More than 100 missiles were aimed at southeast England every day when the operation was at its peak.

16 More than 240 V-1 rockets are fired at targets in England as Germany launches the "Day of Vengeance."

19 The largest aircraft carrier battle in history begins with the Battle of the Philippine Sea in which an estimated 550-645 Japanese aircraft are destroyed over the course of two days.

Summer 1944

■ **ABOVE: Entering from the west side of the town, British and Canadian troops file through the shattered streets of Caen, for the final cleaning-up operations in France.**

June

22 The Russians advance to evict the Germans from Belarus in Operation Bagration.

26 US forces capture Cherbourg, although pockets of resistance continue around the French port for a few days.

29 A planned German offensive near Caen is abandoned after heavy RAF bombing decimated their Panzers.

July

3 The Soviets recapture Minsk but the cost is high with an estimated 80 per cent of the city reduced to rubble.

9 Allied forces, consisting of British and Canadian troops, liberate Caen following heavy German resistance.
   The Pacific island of Saipan is declared secure by American forces. Faced with the humiliation of defeat, the Japanese commanders commit suicide in a cave.

10 Tokyo endures its first bombing raid in more than two years following the introduction of the B-29 that could be launched from Saipan and Tinian.

12 General Field Marshal Walther Model's suggestion to withdraw German forces from Estonia and northern Latvia is dismissed by Hitler.

13 Vilnius in Lithuania is taken by Soviet forces, who launch the Lvov-Sandomierz Offensive with the aim of driving the Germans from eastern Poland and Ukraine.

16 The first batch of the Brazilian Expeditionary Force (the only South American country to supply troops in World War II) arrives in Italy.

17 Field Marshal Rommel is hospitalized with head injuries when Allied fighters near Sainte-Foy-de-Montgommery, France, strafe his staff car.

18 German troops surrender the French town of St. Lô to advancing American forces.

19 The Italian city of Livorno is taken by American troops.

20 A failed attempt by disillusioned German officers to assassinate Hitler takes place in the Rastenburg Assassination Plot. The instigators of the scheme are hanged, their bodies hung on meat hooks, while reprisals are carried out against their families.
   US troops launch an assault on the island of Guam in the Marianas, held by Japanese troops since December 1941.

24 Soviet troops are the first to liberate a concentration camp, Majdanek, in Poland.

25 The British and American troops finally break out of the beachhead in Normandy and begin their advance through France toward Paris.

27 The Battle for the Tannenberg Line begins. It is a series of costly engagements that will claim the lives of tens of thousands of soldiers from both sides.

28 While US troops take Coutances (France), Soviet forces retake Brest-Litovsk (then Poland – now Belarus).

August

1 American troops reach the Lower Normandy town of Avranches.
   An uprising by the Polish Home Army begins against occupying Nazi forces in Warsaw.

ABOVE: The last page of Anne Frank's diary before she was betrayed and arrested.

BELOW: A long line of German prisoners of war march on a field on their way to a POW camp in the Falaise Pocket of Northern France in 1944. They were captured by British and Canadian troops, who escorted them in jeeps.

4 The Allies liberate Florence but not before retreating German forces destroy historic buildings and bridges.

Anne Frank – the teenager whose diary was posthumously published – and her family are betrayed and arrested by the Gestapo in Amsterdam.

7 A German counter-offensive begins in Avranches.

8 A Messerschmitt Me 262 registers a jet fighter's first aerial victory, shooting down a Mosquito PR XVI over Ohlstadt.

15 Operation Dragoon begins with Allied forces landing in the south of France. The invasion involves airborne and amphibious assaults on beaches around Saint-Tropez and Saint-Raphaël.

Allied troops reach Germany's last strategic position in north Italy, the "Gothic Line."

19 Members of the French resistance begin an uprising in Paris.

The Soviets attack Romania, as their Balkan offensive gets under way.

21 The decisive engagement in the Battle of Normandy concludes in the Falaise Pocket when Western Allies encircle 50,000 German troops, effectively ending the Nazis' hold on France.

22 Japanese forces are now in full retreat from India.

25 Allied forces liberate Paris, with General De Gaulle leading a parade through the streets. The city was saved from destruction when German officers refused to carry out Hitler's order to burn the French capital.

28 German forces surrender at Marseilles and Toulon, while General Patton's tanks cross the Marne.

29 The Slovak resistance launches an unsuccessful uprising against Nazi Germany.

31 Soviet forces enter Bucharest following a royal coup that deposes dictator Ion Antonescu. Despite King Michael of Romania denouncing his country's former alliance with Nazi Germany and ceasing military actions against the Allies a week earlier, the Soviets begin an occupation of the country that will last until 1958.

The government of France is handed over to the Free French troops by US forces.

September

2 Allied troops enter Belgium and, within days, cities such as Brussels, Ghent, and Liège are liberated.

5 The Red Army invades Bulgaria who changes allegiance and joins the Soviets three days later as the Axis crumbles.

8 Germany commences its V-2 rocket campaign with strikes against Paris and London.

10 Allied forces begin the battle for Le Havre, the largest port in northern France, with the German garrison surrendering two days later.

15 Soviet forces target German supply routes to cut off troops in Yugoslavia and Greece.

17 Operation Market Garden is set into motion in Holland. Aiming to force an entry route into Germany, the Allies fail in their objective.

19 Finland and the Soviet Union sign an armistice.

22 The Allies' advance through France continues apace and Boulogne becomes the latest city to be liberated.

Fall 1944

■ **ABOVE: The explosion of the USS** *Lexington* **during the Battle of the Coral Sea, 1944.**

September

24 While the Soviet offensive in the Balkans comes to a halt, British troops force their way through to the River Rhine.

25 Allied forces are defeated at the Battle of Arnhem, with more than 2,100 being evacuated from the Netherlands.

26 Estonia is the next country to find itself occupied by the Soviets.

30 Calais is liberated but much of the city lies in ruins following Allied bombardment of German positions.

October

3 A unit of Messerschmitt Me 262 fighters is established near Osnabrück, tasked with combatting US daylight bomber raids over Germany.

4 British forces land on mainland Greece and several Greek islands.

12 The repairs are completed to the docks at Boulogne, thereby aiding the Allies' supply logistics.

14 Allied troops enter the streets of Athens, liberating the Greek capital.

Following his links to the assassination conspiracy against Hitler, Rommel is allowed to commit suicide – as befits a national hero – rather than face a court martial.

15 An armistice is announced between Hungary and the Soviet Union but is rejected by the Hungarian armed forces who continue the fight.

20 The Battle of Leyte begins as US troops land in the Philippines. It will also be the first engagement where the Japanese use kamikaze pilots.

Belgrade is liberated by Yugoslavian partisans and Soviet troops.

21 US forces capture Aachen, which becomes the first German city to fall to the Allies.

German troops will remain fighting on several Greek islands until the following May.

6 As the USS *Lexington* suffers heavy damage at the hands of kamikaze pilots off the Philippines, Roosevelt wins his fourth term as President of the US.

8 Luftwaffe ace Major Walter Nowotny crashes near Osnabrück having claimed his 258 "scalps." The 23-year-old is given a state funeral in Vienna.

12 Allied bombers target *Tirpitz* in Tromsø, Norway, and finally sink the German battleship after numerous attempts.

20 Hitler abandons his headquarters in East Prussia and moves to Berlin.

23 The liberation of France continues with Allied forces succeeding in taking Strasbourg and Metz.

24 B-29 bombers begin to bomb Tokyo from newly constructed air bases in the Mariana Islands.

26 US aircraft from the four carriers escorting convoy TA 1 sink two Japanese warships, *Uranami* and *Kinu*.

28 While German troops are being evacuated from Albania, others are withdrawing in the Netherlands.

November

2 With the Canadian forces' capture of Zeebrugge, the liberation of Belgium is now complete.

4 While the Axis forces in mainland Greece surrender, pockets of

■ **RIGHT: Members of the Special Boat Service were the first British personnel to enter Athens, 1944.**

December

1 In an attempt to hide the atrocities committed by the Nazis, Himmler orders the crematoria at Auschwitz-Birkenau to be dismantled and any evidence disguised.

10 Anglo-Indian troops build the longest Bailey bridge – 1,154 feet (352 m) – across the Chindwin River, the biggest natural obstacle in the Allies' fight to re-occupy Burma.

11 Hitler meets his commanders to emphasize the importance of the forthcoming offensive in the Ardennes.

15 Allied forces cross the border from Alsace, France, into Germany.

16 In response to the invasion of Normandy, the German Army goes on a counter-offensive in what becomes known as the Battle of the Bulge. While casualties on both sides are phenomenally high over the next six weeks, the Allies emerge victorious while the Germans retreat to the "safety" of the Siegfried Line.

Winter 1944-45

December

26 With General Patton in command, the US 3ʳᵈ Army relieves the city of Bastogne, Belgium. Budapest, Hungary, meanwhile, finds itself under siege from Soviet forces.

28 Hitler ignores the advice of his generals and orders the offensive in the Ardennes to be renewed in the face of US advances.

31 The Soviet Union now controls Hungary, who declares war on Germany.

January

1 The Luftwaffe launches its final major offensive in the West with Operation Bodenplatte, an attempt to cripple the Allied air capability in the Low Countries by raiding air bases in Belgium and Holland.

9 US Marines land in Luzon, the main island in the Philippines.

13 The Soviets launch an offensive against German forces on the Eastern Front.

17 Soviet forces liberate Warsaw and set up a Communist-friendly government.

22 The Red Army rapidly advances through Germany, reaching the Oder River, just 90 miles (145 km) away from Berlin.

24 German forces commence their withdrawal from Slovakia. The following day, Germany lays out plans for the evacuation of around 2 million troops through the Baltic.

25 The US bombardment of the Japanese island of Iwo Jima begins in preparation for an invasion.

27 Soviet troops liberate the survivors at Auschwitz.

30 The German liner *Wilhelm Gustloff*, evacuating Germans – both civilian and military – from occupied Poland, is sunk by a Soviet submarine with the loss of more than 9,000 lives.

With the loss of the coal and steel resources of Silesia, it is now almost impossible for the German war machine to keep running.

February

1 Ecuador declares war on Germany. Within the next two weeks, fellow South Americans Paraguay, Peru, and Venezuela follow suit.

4 Roosevelt, Churchill, and Stalin begin discussions of postwar issues at the Yalta Conference in the Crimea.

9 As the last German forces are wiped out to the west of the Rhine, retreating troops demolish the bridge at Chalampé to slow down the Allied advance.

13 The Soviets emerge victorious in the Battle of Budapest, Hungary.

The first of four Allied bombing raids on Dresden is carried out. The justification behind the devastation these cause will remain controversial for decades.

16 The US Navy continues the American bombardment of Japan, with attacks on Tokyo and Yokohama.

19 US Marines gain a foothold in Japan with the invasion of Iwo Jima. The battle rages for five weeks as the Japanese fight to the death with no thought of surrender. In fact, less than one per cent of the Imperial soldiers are taken alive.

25 US and Filipino troops recapture the island of Corregidor in Manila Bay after 10 days of fighting.

March

3 The Philippine capital of Manila is finally liberated from Japanese occupation.

6 Desperate for the supplies of oil in the Lake Balaton region of Hungary, Germany launches Operation Spring Awakening. With the added objective of retaking Budapest, the task is

Spring 1945

March

27 The V-2 missile attacks on Britain come to an end.

29 As Soviet troops cross the border into Austria, Allied forces capture Frankfurt.

April

1 American forces land on the Japanese island of Okinawa and the battle for the island begins. The fighting rages until June 22, with huge loss of life on both sides before an Allied victory.

6 Japan orders all its forces to use kamikaze suicide tactics.
  The Allies launch Operation Grapeshot, an offensive that results in the surrender of German forces in Italy on May 2.

7 The Japanese battleship *Yamato* is sunk by US carrier bombers and torpedo bombers on its way to help with the defense of Okinawa.

11 The Buchenwald death camp is liberated by American troops who are horrified by what they find.

12 President Roosevelt dies of a massive stroke at the age of 63; Vice President Harry S. Truman steps up to the Oval Office.

13 The Soviets enter Vienna and, three days later, begin their final advance to Berlin.

25 Russian forces marching from the east and Allied troops from the west meet at Torgau, Germany.

28 Italian partisans capture Mussolini

and execute him the following day. His body, and that of his mistress and other fascists, is hung upside down in Milan.

29 The Allies liberate the Dachau death camp outside Munich.
  A ceasefire is declared in Italy as all forces surrender.

30 German leader Adolf Hitler commits suicide in his bombproof shelter as the Battle of Berlin rages around him.

May

1 German forces in Italy surrender to the Allies.

2 The Battle of Berlin ends.

4 German forces in northwest Germany, Holland, and Denmark surrender. Admiral Dönitz, who Hitler had nominated as his successor, tries to reach an agreement to surrender to the Western Allies but to be allowed to continue to fight the Soviets. His request is refused.

7 Admiral Dönitz offers an unconditional surrender and the war in Europe ends as the Allies accept Germany's unconditional surrender.

8 The ceasefire comes into effect at 00.01.

9 German forces occupying the Channel Islands surrender.

29 More than 500 B-29 bombers launch a daylight incendiary attack on Yokohama. US bombing

simply too much for the Germans, resulting in a Soviet victory.

7 The Allies cross the Rhine into Germany after the retreating Germans mistakenly leave the Remagen Bridge intact.

11 USAAF B-29s firebomb Nagoya. Many cities in Japan come under heavy bombardment during the month.

20 The Allied forces take Mandalay, Burma.
  Allied forces cross the Rhine at Oppenheim and, the following day, at Wesel – the Allies are now advancing through Germany from all directions.

■ **ABOVE: American generals Omar N. Bradley and George S. Patton meeting among the ruins of Bastogne during the Battle of the Bulge.**

■ **BELOW: A photograph showing troops of the 9th Armored Division of the US 1st Army, heading for the Ludendorff Bridge at Remagen, March 1945.**

raids on Japanese cities had continued throughout the month while Europe was acclimatizing to peace.

June

2 Aircraft from USS *Ticonderoga* target airfields on Kyushu.

5 It is agreed by the Allies that Germany should be divided into four areas.

10 Australian troops land in Borneo, capturing the state of Brunei three days later.

■ **ABOVE: World War II American battleship firing. Okinawa is less than 400 miles from the Japanese home islands and its capture gave the Allies sea and air bases within striking range of the enemy in Japan Formosa and the coastal belt of China.**

■ **BELOW: Corporal William C. LaRue of the Bronx, NY, displays the *New York Post* and the *New York World Telegram* proclaiming "Hitler is Dead,".**

Summer 1945

June

21 The Battle of Okinawa ends with Japan losing more than 100,000 of its original 120,000-strong force.

26 The United Nations Charter is signed by representatives from 50 countries in San Francisco.

July

1 The Battle of Balikpapan, the Allies' last major land action of the conflict, begins on Borneo. The operation is over in three weeks as the Allies claim another victory.

16 The world's first test of a nuclear weapon takes place at Alamogordo in New Mexico by the United States' Manhattan Project.

17 Truman, Churchill, and Stalin meet at the Potsdam Conference where the unconditional surrender of Japan is demanded.

24 The Allies begin the bombing of Kure, destroying the majority of Japan's surviving warships.

26 Churchill is ousted as Prime Minister when the Labour Party wins the United Kingdom's General Election. Clement Attlee is elected as his replacement.

30 The Japanese submarine *I-58* sinks the USS *Indianapolis*.

August

6 The United States drops an atomic bomb on Hiroshima resulting in an estimated 80,000 deaths in the Japanese city and another 70,000 injured.

8 The Soviet Union declares war on Japan and launches an attack on Japanese forces in Manchuria.

9 A second US atomic bomb is dropped on Japan, with between 40,000 and 75,000 people perishing in Nagasaki.

14 Japan unconditionally surrenders to the Allies and peace returns to the world for the first time in six years.

September

2 Japan signs the surrender agreement in Tokyo Bay on board USS *Missouri*.

■ **BELOW: Colonel Paul W. Tibbets Jr., pilot of the *Enola Gay*, the plane that dropped the atomic bomb on Hiroshima, waves from the cockpit before takeoff on August 6, 1945.**